DISCOVERING

DISCOVERING

A USER'S GUIDE TO THE
WORLD OF COLLECTING

Jeanne Frank

Jeanne Frank

THUNDER'S MOUTH PRESS
NEW YORK

Published by
Thunder's Mouth Press
632 Broadway, Seventh Floor
New York NY 10012

Library of Congress Cataloging in Publication Data

Frank, Jeanne
    Discovering art / Jeanne Frank.
        p.   cm.
    Includes bibliographical references.
    ISBN 1-56025-121-2 (pbk.)
        1. Art, Modern—19th century—Themes, motives. 2. Art.
Modern—20th century—Themes, motives. 3. Art—Collectors and
collecting. I. Title.
N6447.F74   1997
709'.0'34—dc21   97-13630
                                                          CIP

ISBN 1-56025-121-2

Manufactured in the United States of America.

Martin Gordon
1939—1995

For Marty, without whose patient teaching and
quixoitic sense of humor, I could never have lived
as exciting and as fulfilling a life
in the world of art.

Acknowledgments

I will be forever grateful to Eugene Ferkauf who took a Yoeman's risk by allowing me the freedom to direct his gallery in my way, mistakes and all.

To those who without their direct involvment and honest criticism this book would have been consigned to the bottom of my Chinese trunk. Geert van der Veen, a good friend, a knowledgeable art dealer, who tackled each page of this manuscript to verify my facts as I went along.

A fine writer and a meticulous editor, Toby Tompkins with his fount of information, on almost all subjects, who not only shaped my run-on sentences, but suggested little known historical information that I of course, took from him.

A dear friend of many years, James Penzi, playwright and lawyer who pens notes to me regularly with one word— WRITE!

My thanks to Ruth Nathan, my agent—without her—so the saying goes—and a terrific lady.

I am fortunate to have so many friends who have encouraged me in my work and who have enriched my life in every way, too many to name them all, but I would like to list a few that belong in this book. Anne-Marie Berger, my prescient assistant, Sylvia Kestenbaum—who for forty years has accepted unconditionally all of my eccentricities and Ricki Polisar, the practical one, who literally pushed me into the gallery to ask for a job. And finally the love from my son, Tom, my daughter Barbara, and my niece Toni.

Contents

INTRODUCTION

"*I* don't know anything about art, but I know what I like."

I have heard this statement repeated over and over again, like a mantra, during the thirty years I've been an art dealer, mostly by successful men and women who have distinguished themselves in other fields. They all have definite opinions about the stock market, politics, the theater, current films, literature and music. But art . . . art seems a mystery so esoteric that to penetrate it they feel they need special knowledge available only to those rarefied individuals with inherited wealth, a tradition of high culture or a degree in art history.

I honestly believe that this uneasy attitude about art has been actively fostered by art critics, reviewers and established galleries. It's hard to understand why the galleries, in particular, try to scare people off art, since they are in business to sell artwork just as car dealers are in business to sell cars. The only reason I can think of is that the gallery owners *themselves* bought into the mystique some time ago and assume that "art experts" make up their only market. Art critics and reviewers are equally guilty, if not more so, of promoting an elitist attitude.

I can recall feeling like a simpleton many years ago, because I wasn't able to make sense out of half the reviews I read in the papers. Today I know better. Now, when I read a critique of an exhibition and the five-syllable words have no relevance to the work, I know the critic hasn't a clue about what the artist is trying to achieve. That's legitimate: it takes time, sometimes years, to comprehend and define an artist's work, and critics can and do get lost occasionally. But instead of stating honestly, "I'm not clear about what this artist is trying to do," some critics go on the attack, or use abstract words and convoluted sentences just to underline their authority as critics. Then again, some simply fall in love with their own literary styles.

I want to add that in any field there are personal grudges, envy and enmity, and these problems exist in the art world as well. Then there are certain reviewers who will jump on the bandwagon if a new artist is heavily promoted by a well-known gallery. These reviewers are afraid of making fools of themselves, in the event that the work eventually takes off and begins to sell for a fortune. There are also critics—I know of a highly respected one—who will savage an artist's work if they don't like his or her politics, or if the work is making a social statement they don't approve of.

I am certainly not condemning *all* critics and reviewers. There are the tried and true, who write from knowledge and from what they sincerely believe, catering to no "isms" or novelty for the sake of novelty. Whether or not I agree with their taste or opinions, I respect their honesty, and I learn from them.

An art review in a newspaper or magazine is not generally written for art historians. Most of us are reasonably intelligent, and if we're literate enough to understand articles on politics or business, we should be able to understand an art review—if it is written to *be* understood. A review written just to serve novelty ultimately serves nobody, neither the public nor the artist.

This book is written to help you gather enough knowledge about art to enjoy it, to feel comfortable with it and, ultimately, to collect it. There are *no* wrong reasons for liking (or disliking) a work of art. We can't legislate what we feel.

There was nothing particular in my background to attract me to art. A friend of mine wanted to be a painter, and I used to visit museums with her. She told me what I was looking at: why Rembrandt was great, who the Dadaists were, what Cubism was and so on. Little by little I began to feel a kind of excitement when I looked at certain works, and eventually I took to wandering through the peaceful rooms of the museum without my guide.

My first love was drawings, even though at that time I couldn't have said why. One Saturday afternoon I ventured into a famous art gallery. It proved to be an experience so intimidating that it was a long time before I worked up the courage to try it again. I don't think I'll ever forget the picture of the young woman seated behind the desk. Her blonde hair was piled high on her head with a loose straggle positioned over each ear, and her makeup was perfectly executed. She resembled every alluring fashion model I'd ever seen in a magazine. Barely glancing up when I walked in, she immediately went back to whatever she was doing, ignoring me. I moved around the spacious room like a trespasser, and I have never felt so self-conscious in my life. The walls were hung with small paintings of bottles and jugs, and while I responded strongly to the austerity of the images—ordinary kitchen objects painted in muted colors against gray backgrounds—I had no idea if they were great art. In my naïveté I assumed they *had* to be, if they hung in a fancy gallery.

They were signed "Morandi." I knew nothing about the artist and wanted to ask questions, but I didn't dare interrupt this elegant creature at the desk. I must have spent *one half hour* in the gallery looking at the work and glancing furtively in the creature's direction, hoping she might look up and offer to help me, or just smile. Nothing. Not a look, not a word, not a sign. Finally I left.

This experience happened in the early sixties, when the general public was just becoming curious about art. The annual street show in Greenwich Village's Washington Square Park was a popular afternoon's excursion. For the first time a few nonexperts began to venture into galleries. Even the auction houses, Christie's and Parke-Bernet (now known as Sotheby's), were a Saturday's adventure. For most people, however, commercial galleries and auction houses remained dangerous: the mystique surrounding them was still too frightening.

But then, after the untimely death of James Rorimer in 1967, Thomas Hoving became director of the Metropolitan Museum in New York. I credit Hoving for cutting through the snobbism and for the first time making the museum and its works fully accessible to the public at large. Although plans for an architectural renovation had been completed in Rorimer's time, when Hoving arrived the Great Hall was still a huge, barren space. There wasn't even a place to sit down. Except to the relatively few people thoroughly sophisticated about art, it was hardly an inviting place. A friend of mine who has been a volunteer at the Metropolitan for over thirty years told me that back in the early sixties, if she wanted to attract a staff member's attention, she'd shout "Yoo hoo!" across the Hall and listen to the echo. It didn't seem to matter to the administration that there were so few visitors.

Hoving began training volunteers on a large scale in 1967, and today there is an information desk manned by friendly people eager to help. He pushed through the renovations: where before there was no place to sit, now, on either side of the Great Hall there are profusions of plants surrounded by circular benches, and fresh flowers flow from niches in the walls. The echo is gone: the atmosphere and aura of the place spell welcome.

Hoving hired Harry Parker to direct an educational art program, and in 1968 he convinced Diana Vreeland to create a delightful Costume Institute. In deference to working people unable to come during the day, he kept the museum open Tuesday evenings until 8:30.

Hoving brought in blockbuster shows with a fanfare of publicity. One of the most famous of them, in 1969, was "Harlem on My Mind," a controversial exhibition which created a sensation in the papers, on television and on radio, and brought in a brand-new public, many of whom had never set foot inside a museum. The show took up thirteen galleries of the vast museum and celebrated almost every aspect of Harlem from the twenties through the early sixties. There were small and life-size photographs of celebrated, creative black people; the recorded voices of Malcolm X, Joe Louis and many others; the music of Billie Holiday, Aretha Franklin and Marian

Anderson. "Harlem on My Mind" brought 247,000 visitors.
Hoving made the Metropolitan Museum a people's cultural
paradise, a down-to-earth populist center for ordinary people
to visit—and they did! He humanized not only the Metropolitan, but museums throughout the country, partly by exchanging traveling shows with other institutions, and partly
by his own energetic example, which inspired museum direc-
tors in other cities.

In the sixties people were beginning to feel less threatened
by art. There was money to spare, and many thought about
collecting "real" works of art for their homes. It was a heady
time, and I was part of it, in a uniquely American way.

During the late fifties and early sixties department stores
began setting up art galleries. There were three major stores
which began the innovation: Sears, Roebuck in Chicago, J. L.
Hudson in Detroit and E. J. Korvette on Long Island, New
York. It was a populist experiment, and very exciting: for the
first time fine art was made available to the general public.

I lived on Long Island at the time Eugene Ferkauf, who
created E. J. Korvette as the first discount department store
in the country, opened a penthouse gallery in his Douglaston
branch. He devoted about 3,000 square feet to the gallery.
Vitrines for the display of small sculptures and drawings were
set into paneled walls, and although he carried some paintings, the walls themselves were hung primarily with works on
paper—watercolors, gouaches, collages, etchings, lithographs, etc. (I'll define these terms in a later chapter on
graphics.) The lighting equaled that of any small, well-
designed museum. It was truly a lovely space.

A small area was set aside for paperback books, most of
them published by Skira, a Swiss art publishing house. Skira
books boasted striking covers and faithful color reproductions. Some volumes covered the life and work of a specific

6

world-famous artist, with biographical and critical notes; others dealt with various movements in the history of art—Impressionism, Fauvism and so on. They were small, well bound, comprehensive, easy to read and, above all, inexpensive.

In 1965 a change in my life sent me to E. J. Korvette to ask for a job in the Douglaston gallery. By that time I had learned enough to recognize the work of Picasso, Chagall, Miró, Braque, Baskin, Giacometti, Rouault and other important artists of the twentieth century. The manager of the gallery hired me, at the minimum wage of the time, around three dollars an hour. I worked like a plowhorse. I read every book in the gallery in order to stay one day ahead of what I needed to know, I stayed up late at night doing further research on the artists on exhibit and during the days I did my best to share my enthusiasm with the customers. And I loved every minute of it.

After a year Mr. Ferkauf offered me a promotion to director and buyer for his gallery. I told him he was mad. The only experience I had ever had in the art world had been the year in his gallery.

He said, "First, you don't call your boss mad. If I'm willing to take a chance on you, you ought at least to take a chance on yourself."

So I did—with the proviso that if I failed I could get my three-dollar-an-hour job back. He agreed. Although I didn't feel qualified for the position, I had one advantage: the staff assigned to the gallery had originally been in Shirts and Refrigerators.

The people who shopped at Korvette's were predominately from Long Island, and Saturday was particularly busy down in the main store. It was the day to pick up groceries, buy clothes for the children, new tires, maybe a refrigerator (or a shirt), whatever. Little by little customers began taking the escalator up to see what was on the top floor. Advertising in the New York papers had begun bringing in a few dealers and collectors, some from as far away as Canada, but most people whose curiosity prompted them up the escalator had never been in an art gallery. The first time around, they would look, shake their heads, and walk out. But each week, more and more of them came back, after they had finished their shopping downstairs. I soon realized they were dying to ask questions, but felt self-conscious about approaching anyone. Recalling the intimidation I felt when I made my own first gallery visit, I went by what I would have wanted then: basic information.

I placed a placard on an easel near the entrance, which explained the various techniques of the works on display—etchings, lithographs, linoleum cuts, monoprints and so forth—and defined the penciled numbers in the margins of the pictures. Under each work I pasted a card giving the artist's name, the medium of the work and the price.

The crowds grew week by week, and I convinced Mr. Ferkauf—it wasn't hard to do, he loved his gallery—to let me hire a staff which had a little more knowledge of art than the Refrigerators and Shirts people. The initially timid visitors gained confidence when they realized they could ask questions and get friendly, expert answers. After repeated trips and many discussions, some of the visitors actually began buying drawings, graphics or a book.

The same people returned week after week, often bringing friends. Eventually the regular Korvette customers were joined by people from all over Long Island and from New York City as well, people who came to the Douglaston branch specifically to visit the gallery. We began to put on monthly openings and special exhibits—the first show ever of Giacometti's graphic work was a highlight—and we mounted group exhibitions of the work of young artists, some who today exhibit throughout the country. Thanks to the placard on the easel and the cards next to every work, no one hesitated to ask questions. The openings were mobbed.

When the late Abe Chanin, the lecturer for the Museum of Modern Art, came to the gallery to give the first in a series of talks, the maintenance staff set up twenty-five chairs and told me to call if I needed more. Over one hundred and fifty people showed up!

I remember one woman in particular, a tiny lady in a blue coat who used to come in every Saturday promptly at 11 AM carrying a heavy shopping bag in each hand. She'd leave her bags next to my desk and do a fast trot around the room until she arrived, every time, at an aquatint titled *Qui ne se grime pas* (*The One Who Does Not Wear a Mask*), often referred to as *The Clown*, from the *Miséraire* portfolio by Rouault. After gazing at the picture for several minutes she'd turn, smile at no one in particular, pick up her parcels and leave. But one morning she came in for what the staff and I called her "Saturday fix," and found the picture was gone.

She rushed over to my desk, highly affronted, and asked why the Rouault wasn't there. I told her it had been sold.

"We *sell* the pictures we have here," I said, as gently as I could.

She looked at me, disbelieving, and her eyes filled with tears. Without a word she turned and left. We never saw her again. Privately, I wished the Rouault hadn't sold, for her sake.

The people who came to the Korvette gallery were from many walks of life: doctors, lawyers, mechanics, teachers, clerks, businessmen. A man who owned a dry cleaning establishment never missed a week in the three years I worked there—and in time he opened his own art gallery on 57th Street in Manhattan.

All these years later I still bump into people on the street, at the theater, in a gallery or an auction house, who stop me and ask, "Do you remember me from Korvette's?" Some of them tell me that because of their first exposure to art at the store, their favorite pastime is wandering through museums and galleries. Others have gone further, starting their own collections. For a few, art has become an all-consuming passion. Because of the E. J. Korvette gallery, they tell me, art has become a satisfying and fulfilling addition to their lives.

Sadly, fine art galleries in department stores are almost extinct today. The function of a department store has nothing to do with special commodities like works of art, which can hardly be marked down like socks if they don't sell. So it goes—it was great while it lasted.

People still tell me today that they would love to know something about art, and might even like to buy a painting, but they remain uncomfortable in galleries. "How do I know what I'm doing?" they ask me. "What if I buy a painting that isn't good art? I wouldn't know the difference." The art experience still remains intimidating for them, when it should be pleasurable and fun.

I can only repeat what I learned from selling art in a department store: you don't need an academic background to enjoy art, appreciate it, distinguish quality from junk and eventually acquire enough knowledge and self-confidence to start your own collection. I promise you that by the time you finish this book you will be comfortable and knowledgeable enough to buy a work of art without apologies. You will know what you like, and will have enough basic information to know *why* you like it.

1

GETTING YOUR FEET WET

I think the best introduction to art is to stroll through a museum. Perhaps you've thought about buying a painting or sculpture one day, but have put it off because you didn't know how to begin, where to go, what to ask. Well, browsing in your local museum can be a most delightful and illuminating experience, provided you're armed with some basic facts and a few suggestions.

Begin by spending a free hour or two just getting a feel for the place. Look at what's on display . . . possibly a special exhibition of ancient art, a show of contemporary paintings or a sampling of the museum's permanent collection. Stay only as long as you're enjoying it, and when you're full, *leave*. For me, one or two hours is enough. By then I've absorbed all I can, and after that it just becomes one big blur.

I used to watch museumgoers study a single painting for

what seemed like an age, and I'd ask myself, "What are they seeing that I don't?", certain that there was some critical ingredient lacking in my intelligence. Finally one day I encountered two women standing in hushed reverence before a painting that I liked, and I overheard one say to the other, "Look at that line, and the curve on the right, the sense of space." It was then I realized that seeing a painting in terms of its *parts* was not my way. My own response is sparked by my *overall* impression. The total image either sings to me or it doesn't.

Gertrude Stein, the American writer who lived in Paris and was one of Picasso's and Matisse's first patrons, advised, "When in a museum, walk slowly but keep walking." I subscribe to her counsel, but you may react differently, finding that if a particular work catches your attention, you prefer to stop and take some time to study it more carefully. However you feel and however you respond to a work of art is *your* way. There is no "supposed to" when it comes to looking at art.

Nor do you have to like a given piece just because someone else says it's a masterwork or tells you how famous the artist is. Trust yourself, and don't take your museum visit too seriously by assuming that everything you see is great art just because it's in a museum. Taste in art, as in everything, is personal, and it changes throughout life, based on repeated exposure and widening experience. Keep *looking:* knowledge will come in time. If you feel formal training is important, there are museum lectures and adult education courses you can attend. I've been on some wonderful weekend art tours and well-organized day trips sponsored by museums. I remember a particular trip to the Barnes Collection, outside Philadelphia, and another to one of the best exhibitions of German Expressionists I've ever seen, organized by Serge Sabarsky at the Nassau County Museum. Both tours were sponsored by an adult education class.

Back to your museum: for now let's drift through and try to be aware only of gut reactions. Look at the shapes, the colors in many different kinds of pictures, from familiar landscapes, still-lives and portraits to those big blobs that signify nothing you can recognize, let alone relate to. The more art you see, the more you'll learn to define your own taste.

13

As an experiment, try jotting down the names of the artists whose work appeals to you. After a time you'll find that the artists and the works all have something in common. The common factor may involve color: maybe you favor bright, vibrant hues, or perhaps you prefer the subtler, more muted tones. Or you may discover that you are attracted to a certain subject matter, regardless of the style in which it is executed.

One day during my own early explorations I was sauntering through the Impressionist and Post-Impressionist galleries in New York's Metropolitan Museum, wondering if there was a pattern to the kind of paintings I liked. I had a notebook and, following my immediate reactions, wrote down the names Vincent van Gogh, Pierre Auguste Renoir and Gustave Caillebotte. Although all three worked in France during the latter part of the nineteenth century, their works could not have been more dissimilar. Van Gogh's portrait of the postman's wife was painted in the passionate colors of the blinding southern sun; Renoir's delicate child, her soft features framed by a brimmed bonnet, was rendered in pale blues and pinks; Caillebotte's man and woman on a rainy day in Paris, he holding an umbrella, were done almost in gray-scale. I loved all three paintings, and the common element, when I finally figured it out, was that each of them had human subjects. I like pictures of people, simple as that.

Try it yourself. Select three works of art—paintings or sculptures—which appeal to you, and ask yourself why. Your answer may be as simple as mine was: perhaps all three are landscapes, still-life's or portraits. My discovery that I loved paintings of the human figure, regardless of the medium or the technique, formed the foundation for my developing taste in art. The more I looked at different kinds of pictures, the more I learned. As my taste expanded with experience, I discovered abstract art and developed an intense interest in sculptors' drawings and non-figurative sculpture.

Now, many years later, I can still recall my feeling of awe at being seated next to the late James Johnson Sweeny at a dinner party. Mr. Sweeny was the first director of the Guggenheim Museum in New York, and later became director of the Houston Fine Arts Museum. Upon his retirement he was asked to go to Israel to be art advisor to the Israel Museum in Jerusalem. During the dinner I asked him if he had a preference for abstract or figurative art. He didn't hesitate for a moment: "It doesn't matter. I've no preference. It's either good art or bad art." James Sweeny supported and promoted many young, talented avant-garde artists, and was most definitely an iconoclast in the sometimes stuffy museum world. The story goes that when he was director of the Houston Museum, he bought a large, abstract Chillida sculpture and had it cemented deep into the ground, so that, as he said, "if they wanted to get rid of it, they couldn't dig it up." The tale may be apocryphal, but it has a Sweeny quality. And his judgment proved right over and over again: "It's either good art or bad art." That, in essence, is what *art* is all about.

I've started you out in a museum rather than in a commercial gallery for a number of reasons. Museums have no axes to grind: the work displayed is not for sale, except in unusual instances. The exhibitions are set up to provide an interested public with a relaxed, peaceful environment in which to view works of art at leisure (this goes for all museums, not just the great institutions in big cities). For special exhibitions the larger museums provide audio tapes on which curators discuss the featured work. And even in smaller museums, there are trained volunteer docents to guide you through.

A large museum is divided into a number of rooms, wings and display spaces. These areas are often referred to as "galleries," and, in general, each gallery is devoted to a different period and style of art. The grand museums in big cities have enough space and large enough collections to dedicate a separate gallery to every phase of the entire history of art, from artifacts carved in bone and stone by our earliest ancestors, to the work of the most contemporary artists. Smaller museums around the country separate the different periods of art as well, doing their best to demonstrate the continuity of art history.

Scattered throughout the United States are other museums, which concentrate on *specific* kinds of art. The Delaware Art Museum, for example, is celebrated for its collection of Early American paintings. The Cleveland Museum has a glorious collection of Oriental art. In New York City, where I live, the Smithsonian/Cooper Hewitt Crafts Museum features exciting exhibits of everything from antique furniture through fabric design to unusual birdhouses.

You may find that although you live in a smaller city than New York, Chicago, Houston, Cleveland or Los Angeles, your museum is known throughout the country for certain special holdings. Perhaps it boasts a collection of rare antique furniture, or it might possess a single great work of art which the big-city museums would die for. In Milwaukee, where I was born and raised, the Milwaukee Public Museum is recognized for its Indian artifacts and its impressive panoramic scenes of early Indian life in Wisconsin. Marion, Pennsylvania, a suburb of Philadelphia, houses the Barnes Collection, one of the most magnificent collections of Impressionist and Post-Impressionist paintings and drawings in the world. The DeMenil Museum in Houston has a matchless accumulation of Magritte and Léger paintings; the Kimball Museum, Dallas/Fort Worth, has a very choice collection of twentieth-century artworks; the Everson Museum in Syracuse, New York, is world-famous for its ceramics; the Albright Knox Art Gallery in Buffalo specializes in American twentieth-century artists. The list goes on and on: my point is that you don't have to travel to one of the grand institutions to "get your feet wet." Chances are there's a fine museum not far from where you live.

And there's always the possibility of making a thrilling discovery in an unlikely place. Some years ago I visited friends in the south of France and found, almost by accident, a tiny jewel of a museum in St. Tropez. I was wandering along the sea promenade when, at its very end, I spied a small building bearing a sign that read, *Exhibition: Metzinger*. I went in, and was astonished to find a room of fine Cubist paintings by the French artist Metzinger. I was even more astonished by the little museum's permanent collection: works by Derain, Vlaminck, Chagall, Miró, and other giants of twentieth-century art, all of outstanding quality. I don't think I have ever seen finer paintings by Vlaminck and Derain in their Fauvist periods. I asked who had financed the place and donated the collection, but nobody seemed to know. I've been back several times since, and each time I've asked an official at the St. Tropez Town Hall for more information about the museum. So far I've only gotten an assortment of Gallic shrugs. Perhaps the lucky French simply take such treasures for granted.

There is magic everywhere. Explore your own back yard! You never can tell what you might find.

Whether you live in a small city or a big one, you'll find advance notices about traveling shows in your local papers or magazines. For instance, if the director of your museum is interested in the American artist Edward Hopper and finds out that a traveling retrospective exhibition of Hopper's work is planned, he'll bid for it to stop at his museum. Mounting a traveling show in a small museum can be expensive: your director will be responsible for shipping expenses and insurance, as well as the cost of installing the exhibition. But if the show is important, even if the museum's immediate funds are inadequate, it is quite likely that one or more of its trustees will raise the necessary money or make up the expenses personally.

Museums have long benefited from the generosity of local philanthropists, men and women of wealth and taste who have built up remarkable art collections during their lifetimes and often leave everything to their local museums—every director's dream. Museums in both large and small cities depend heavily upon their wealthy patrons, who are invaluable when it comes to raising money from other individuals, over and above their own contributions.

Museums also promote memberships as a fund-raising device. Usually a museum membership costs very little per year, and it is a good idea to join. As a member of your museum, you'll be admitted to special exhibitions, lectures and other events. You'll receive a newsletter giving you advance notice of projected programs. And if your museum charges admission, you'll get a discount. But the best thing about a museum membership is that it will give you a sense of *participation* in the ongoing life of the place: as a member, each time you visit you'll feel you belong.

Museums, at least the larger ones, provide a grand overview of the main currents in the history of art, and reveal the essential living history of human culture. While you wander through the various galleries of your museum, notice the differences between the works of subsequent centuries, from the formal religious art of the European Romanesque period, through the more secular art of the Gothic period, to the fully figured images, shown in perspective, of the Renaissance. The subject matter—lives of the saints, incidents from the life of Christ—remains the same. But how wonderful to see how successive generations of artists treated it!

Although this book deals primarily with the art of the late nineteenth century through the major figures of the twentieth, repeated museum visits will give you some sense that all periods, constantly changing and evolving, are part of a continuous process. Each period relates to the following one, and reveals much about the living history of humanity. Museums provide you with privacy and anonymity: you can begin your journey into art responsible to nothing but your own evolving taste. They are the ideal places in which to "get your feet wet."

18

2

COMMERCIAL GALLERIES, PRIVATE DEALERS AND AUCTION HOUSES

*O*nce you've introduced yourself to the riches your museum has to offer and have begun to develop a feeling for what appeals to you, pay a visit to the art galleries in your city—you'll probably find there are more of them than you thought. There's no better way to educate yourself in the culture of our time than to see the work of contemporary artists. If you encounter a green string attached to a blank canvas hanging on the wall, or a plain old rock on the floor, you might ask yourself, "Is this art?" I can't answer that, although I've been asked the question myself so many times. You may think it's rubbish, but someone else might say, "How innovative, an ordinary green string, but look what it does to the space around it!" I'll use the cliché, "Beauty is in the eye of the beholder."

Look around the gallery, just as if you were in a museum.

If you see a work of art that intrigues you, ask the owner or a gallery staffer whatever questions come to mind.

"I like this painting. It's different from the kind of art I usually like, but I like its colors. Will you tell me something about the piece and the artist? Is this the artist's first show? How much is this particular painting? If you have other work by the artist which isn't on display, may I see it?"

These are all valid questions—no doubt you'll think of more—and you should feel free to ask them.

A word of caution: I strongly suggest that you *never* make a final judgment of an artist's work by one piece, or even by a single exhibition. The work of art you fall in love with and want to live with will mean much more to you if you know the body of the artist's work. Not every painting an artist does is of the same quality, even if it's by Monet, Renoir or Picasso: even famous artists had off days.

How will you know the difference between a good and a mediocre work by the same artist? That's a big question, and there's only one answer I know of: keep looking and looking at as many pieces by the artist as you can find. Compare the differences from piece to piece. Eventually you'll get a feel for the overall quality of the artist's work, and you'll be able to discern the quality of a particular painting. You'll feel it through your eyes—that's the only way I know how to explain it.

When you first begin to visit galleries, it's a good idea to take out a subscription to an art magazine. *Art News* and *Art in America* are both good ones. The magazines cover museum exhibitions and gallery shows throughout the country, and often include information on European galleries and museums as well. Some galleries advertise in the magazines, with illustrations of their upcoming exhibitions. Many of the reviews and critiques you'll encounter are interesting and en-

20

lightening—and some are unreadable from the first sentence to the last. Remember, if *you* can't understand an art review, there's probably nothing in it worth worrying about. The good art magazines are generally free of intimidating art jargon, though. They are inexpensive, and they'll provide you with a condensed general picture of what's going on from month to month in the art world.

In addition to the monthly magazines, most galleries in big cities will have a small publication called a gallery guide available at their front desks. The guide lists current exhibitions in each of the galleries in your city, with dates, addresses and phone numbers. Gallery guides are free: take one with you.

Finally, most galleries have a visitor's book to sign, so that you will receive information about future shows, with dates and times of openings and so on. Openings are usually every four to six weeks, between five and seven o'clock. After I became less intimidated by the atmosphere in the public galleries, I began attending openings and meeting people. Openings are generally relaxed affairs: everybody stands around exchanging information about other shows in town. I've made more than one good art friend at openings, people with whom I now go regularly to museums and galleries.

If it happens that while you are looking at the art in a gallery, the director or a staff member asks you what you are interested in, there's nothing wrong with saying, "I don't know yet. I'm just looking and enjoying myself." The dealer, if he or she is smart, will regard you as a potential client, and therefore it will be in her or his financial interest to help you as much as possible. Remember that art dealing is a very precarious way to make a living. There's no steady income, no weekly salary. The majority of established, respected dealers did not go into business just to make their fortunes. If money were the only consideration, they would have become stockbrokers. Most dealers enter the dicey field because they love art. I know that's why I did: I loved being surrounded by works of art, and I wanted eventually to own some myself.

Most of the dealers I know had been in other businesses first, and had become art collectors. But they liked being part of the art world so much that in the end they couldn't resist opening a gallery to buy and sell what they loved. One stockbroker left Wall Street to become a successful dealer in Early American art; another dealer with a great gallery and equally great taste had been a shirt manufacturer. I could go on and on. And I know two or three second-generation art dealers.

You'll find that when you ask questions that show your interest, most often you'll get friendly, enthusiastic responses. But remember, you are in a *store*. Take the dealer's enthusiasm with a grain of salt: what he thinks is great, you may hate.

Certain commercial galleries maintain a "stable." This means they exhibit, sell and promote the work of a group of artists the dealers believe have the creative promise which will, in time, contribute substantial and significant work to the ongoing story of art. Some of these dealers offer their young artists a stipend so that they can buy their materials and pay their rent. In return for the stipend, the artist gives the dealer the exclusive right to exhibiting and selling his or her work.

The stable system goes back to the end of the nineteenth century. In Paris, Paul Durand Ruel not only championed the so-called avant-garde artists, but bought the work of Monet, Manet and Pissarro to keep them going—in the beginning he managed to sell their paintings only very occasionally, to his regular clients. Later, Ambroise Vollard became the exclusive dealer for Renoir, Degas, Pissarro, Sisley and Cézanne, among other Impressionists and Post-Impressionists. Vollard sold their work to anyone he could convince to buy it. There were two or three other dealers during the period who believed in these artists, but my point is to suggest how difficult it was, in the beginning, to sell the work of the painters we have come to love and revere today.

In 1907 Daniel Henry Kahnweiler opened his gallery in Paris. He represented only young and then-unknown artists: Pablo Picasso, Juan Gris, Fernand Léger, Georges Braque, Maurice Vlaminck and André Derain. They were artists in whom he had great faith, and he supported them through thick and thin.

The idea of a stable of artists existed in America as well, and still does. From the twenties until she died, Edith Halpert's stable consisted of the Americans Charles Sheeler, John Sloan, Marsden Hartley, Thomas Hart Benton and others who became known for the work they did for the WPA during the thirties. Their work presented the social landscape of that time: subjects included factories, construction sites, farmers and laborers.

Another dealer, Betty Parsons, came later, and is remembered for introducing the young, mainly abstract artists of the forties and fifties—among them Adolph Gottlieb, Mark Rothko, David Smith, Barnett Newman and Clyfford Still—all of whom have since become prominent in the world of art.

There are other dealers here and in most Western countries who support artists emotionally as well as financially. The stable system depends upon dealers who work hard and keep faith with the artists they represent. It usually takes years before the work of promotion and support finally pays off—and many times it never does.

In the late seventies, into the eighties, the art world as many of us knew it changed markedly. We'd always been serious and excited about our world, but in the past money hadn't been its be-all and end-all: "hype" had not been a regular part of our vocabulary. But then the economy boomed, and suddenly there was a lot of loose money around. A great many new collectors, young and inexperienced, appeared, and they went to galleries newly opened by people equally inexperienced, who had decided art was a way to get rich quick. The art market became a money-oriented business. Even the formerly conservative auction houses were affected: buying, at whatever price, and whether or not you knew what you were doing, was the "in thing." Suddenly artists who had barely begun to define their own visions were selling their work for hundreds of thousands of dollars to uninitiated, unsophisticated collectors.

The boom didn't last long, of course. The recession of the 1990s closed down the flashy new galleries, and some fine old reputable ones folded too. A number of collectors who bought into the mad fever of speculation have lived to see their trendy pictures fall through the floor in value.

There's an anecdote about the eighties concerning a rich collector hosting a dinner party. Suddenly a crash was heard from the living room, where he had hung a painting which incorporated ceramic objects glued to the canvas. The glue had suddenly given way and all the ceramics fell to the floor. The artist in question has since gone on to other media.

Yet with all the pretentiousness of the eighties, something wonderful and positive came out of the period. With art suddenly a popular commodity, new artists—good, bad or indifferent—got a chance to have their work seen. During this high-flying period I discovered the work of many talented people with strong personal visions—artists I predict will one day become revered. It wasn't all bad.

Aside from galleries with their own stables of young artists, or galleries handling artists who have become internationally famous in their own lifetimes, there are galleries which own the exclusive rights to the work of dead artists. They don't necessarily own the works themselves, but by arrangement with the artists' estates, they control the exhibition and sale of unsold work held by the estates. Over the years the work of celebrated artists changes hands many times. If deceased artists have been recognized as important "masters" during their lifetimes, their art may command much higher prices than that of living artists, simply because the supply is finite. I say "may," because even the work of a dead "master" goes in and out of fashion.

The term "master" is ambiguous, especially today, when it is used so freely and indiscriminately. I believe a "master" is an artist whose work makes a universal statement about the condition of humanity; who has created a body of work that enables the viewer to attain a new and unique vision of the world; who has attained a high level of technical skill; and, perhaps most importantly, one whose work has survived the test of time—the scrutiny of thousands of knowledgeable people over years, even generations. Time is the ultimate arbiter of "master" status. Just as Shakespeare, Beethoven or Frank Lloyd Wright survived the trends of their own periods, we can claim the same universality for Michelangelo, Rembrandt and Goya.

William Rubin, who retired from his position as director of the Museum of Modern Art in New York in 1996, told an interviewer, "The number of artists from any period that after fifty or a hundred years seem worth preserving, is very small. All you can do is follow your instincts. We are all blind swimmers in the end."

In recent years living artists who have produced a sizable

body of original, significant work have been hailed as "modern masters" by the galleries who represent them. Remember, gallery owners have a vested interest in claiming "modern master" status for their chosen artist: their belief in the artist's greatness is related to their own taste and bank account. Time may prove them right, or may prove them to be quite blind. Many artists lauded as "masters" in their own time are today barely footnotes in the history of art. And others who were ignored during their lifetimes are acknowledged posthumously as "masters," or at least recognized as very fine artists.

"Old master" paintings—roughly, European works from the fifteenth through the seventeenth centuries—are by now so rare that when one in good condition (which means that it hasn't been over-painted, re-painted, lacquered over) does turn up for sale, it will go for tens of millions. "Modern master" paintings by living or recently deceased artists may also sell in the millions, but I suggest that you let your own taste guide you, rather than buying a "modern master" as an investment. It's a high-stakes gamble at best, as many so-called art investors have found to their cost. But if you do find a "modern master" whose work you have fallen in love with (and can afford), take this advice to heart: don't buy a third-rate piece for its signature. And if the work is of museum quality, it will rarely be a bargain. The finest artists have all painted "good pictures" which are not necessarily masterpieces. But because they are worthy examples of the artists' general body of work, they are coveted by museums and major collectors seeking to round out their permanent collections, and they won't come cheap.

Great artists, even the likes of Monet, Cézanne and Picasso, have also done very secondary work, and even just plain bad paintings, pieces they'd probably destroy themselves if they were alive today. But because of the almighty signature, bad work by good artists can still command a hefty price in the market. My advice is, if you cannot afford a work truly characteristic of an established artist, buy the best work of a new one.

For me, quality is the key word, and as your knowledge deepens, you'll develop your own solid instincts for recognizing it. Visit the galleries in your city. Look at the work of your local artists—for "local" certainly doesn't mean "lesser." If you happen upon an artist whose technique and content attract you, go ahead and buy something. Follow the artist's career. I have done that several times in my professional life. It is always exciting to sponsor a young artist. I feel great when I think I may have discovered a budding "master" (and I'm always convinced that I have).

Artists come from everywhere: big cities, tiny villages and everything in between. Most have struggled and almost starved before they were recognized even in a small way. In the twentieth century almost all of the artists acknowledged as "modern masters" owe their success to courageous collectors and dealers who found something extraordinary in their early work and followed their instincts.

There's an anecdote in James Mellows's book *The Charmed Circle* which illustrates my point. Gertrude Stein befriended young, unknown artists she felt were talented, and collected their work. She encouraged and bought the work of Cézanne, Denis, Juan Gris, the young Matisse and Picasso, to name only a few of the avant-garde artists of her time. When Dr. Claribel Cone and her sister Etta, old friends of Gertrude from Baltimore, visited her in Paris, she took them to Picasso's studio and persuaded them to buy a few drawings from the struggling artist for two or three dollars a piece. These were the drawings that became the foundation of the world-famous Cone Collection at the Baltimore Museum.

Private dealers make up another category in the art world—
28 | I have been one myself for many years. For the most part we work out of our homes or offices and are available only by appointment. Since it's almost impossible to get started without having a public track record, so that we are known to other dealers, galleries, museum curators and collectors, most of us have worked in or owned a public gallery at one time— my own track record came from my years as director of E. J. Korvette's gallery.

Private dealers list themselves in art directories, art magazines and in the art sections of newspapers. A well-established private dealer also relies on word-of-mouth within the art world. Because we don't have space in which to mount shows of unknown artists, we usually handle the art of the proven, the known. Occasionally I do find an artist whose work I believe in. Like Vollard, I try to convince my regular clients to buy my discovery's work, and I'll often try to find a public gallery willing to give the work a wider exposure. But my main source is the work I buy from private persons (collectors who do not want the world to know their business), from the estates of dead artists and from other private dealers who have acquired a work of art that does not fit their venues, but is to my taste.

Most private dealers are also collectors. It is hardly possible for the majority of us to own everything we hang in our premises, but I feel a substantial and serious private dealer is one who has backed his or her taste with some of their own money, building up a choice, if small, collection of quality work. People who want to sell their own collections, and those

in a financial position to buy them, are naturally more inclined to trust a fellow collector of first-rate work.

Many people choose to deal privately with a single person
who guides them in building a collection. I like the one-on-
one relationship: it's closer than the formality one often en-
counters in a public gallery. The collector sees the work in my
home, and we have time for talking with no interference. In
this way the new client receives a broader education in art
than he or she would otherwise. And because of the relaxed
atmosphere I quickly learn my client's tastes, and thus am in
a better position to help them build a cohesive collection.
Some clients have come to me for so many years that we've
become more than business acquaintances, and have developed lasting friendships. I think this is generally the situation
with private dealers who have been around for a while.

An appointment with a private dealer should be no more
intimidating than a visit to a public gallery. Just because you
are in someone's home, you certainly don't have to like everything you see. You have a perfect right to say, "Thank you,
but this is not what I'm looking for," and leave.

Last we come to auction houses—*not* good places to buy art,
unless you have a great deal of experience. Art auctions, in
which thousands and millions of dollars change hands, are for
people who, first and foremost, know the *current market value*
of the works being offered. The art market fluctuates, depending on the state of the overall economy and a host of
other factors: the reputation of a given artist, for example,
can rise or sink over a period of only a few years, based on
completely unpredictable shifts in public taste. All too often

the new collector, not yet savvy to what is going on in the art market, will get carried away by the excitement that often attends auctions, and buy on impulse.

I will never forget what happened to two women I saw at an afternoon auction some time ago. They appeared to have come just for the fun of spending a few hours seeing what an auction was like, probably with no prior intention of buying. A framed lithograph was placed on the auctioneer's easel, and each woman must have thought it would look great over her sofa. They began bidding madly against each other, while the rest of the room watched in some disbelief. The final sum was outrageous, and the "lucky winner" hadn't a clue that the same lithograph could be bought in a gallery for less than half of what she paid at auction—nor did she seem to realize that fifteen percent of the purchase price would be tacked on for the auction house.

In the eighties, during the height of the boom, a friend who had inherited an enormous painting by a tenth-rate artist asked me to sell it for her. I told her I couldn't. My credibility as a dealer would go down the drain if I even tried, and besides, even if I did find a buyer, if *that* person ever wanted to resell the thing, I wouldn't have the foggiest notion where to find another buyer. Put it in auction, I said, and if you get a few thousand dollars, celebrate! After all, the painting was so huge the canvas alone would have been worth a thousand.

But it was the eighties, and the Japanese were buying mediocre art, the kind of stuff the French had sold a generation ago to unsuspecting, unlearned Americans. My friend took my advice: at the auction the piece sold for $55,000! Now that the Japanese have come to recognize good Western art, I've often wondered where this monstrosity will finally end up.

An auction can indeed be wonderfully exciting, especially when a major piece or a whole collection goes on the block.

Dealers and experienced collectors who regularly attend auctions know the factors which determine the value of a given work: the physical condition of the work; whether or not it has been restored, and if so, how much restoration has been done; whether it is an early or late work by the artist (with certain artists early is not always better). At any auction bidding is a specialized skill, but at small country auctions you can participate in the fun without getting seriously burned. At big auctions involving thousands and millions of dollars, things are considerably more dangerous. *Always* be sure to read the small print in the auction catalogues.

Go to the big auctions as a spectator. Better still, attend the viewings of the pieces coming up. All auction houses exhibit the work that will go on the block anywhere from four days to a week before the actual sale date. If it's a major sale, you will find under one roof the kind of great art you can ordinarily see only in a museum. The pre-auction viewing, like the gallery opening, is a wonderful place to meet and talk to people. If you do find a drawing or a graphic work that you like enough to want to bid on, ask to have it removed from its frame so that you can see its condition. Check to see if the piece is torn, or if someone has folded in its edges to make it fit into a cherished old frame. This request is perfectly legitimate. Knowledgeable people will not bid on anything at auction unless they can satisfy themselves completely about its condition.

I realize I have been putting a lot of emphasis on caution in this section, and I don't mean to scare you off actually *buying* a work of art. You've done your browsing, you've gotten your feet wet. You've picked up knowledge by visiting museums, public galleries, private dealers and auction houses. Above all, you've made important discoveries about your own taste. Knowing what you like—and by now, having

31

a good idea why you like it—if you run into a work of art that speaks to you, proceed with confidence! "I'm buying this piece because I like it—the color, the mood, the way it makes me feel. I want to own it." That's all the justification you need: if you can afford it, by all means buy it and enjoy it. And remember, don't make a permanent commitment to "I love it" or "I hate it." What you don't like today you may love tomorrow. If you've bought a piece only to find it goes stale on you in time, you haven't made a mistake, you've *grown*. Here's a suggestion I've followed myself: rehang the piece in the guestroom or the bathroom—or offer it to your kids. Have no regrets: you will take another look at it one day and smile.

In the following chapters I will define, very briefly, some of the more widely known movements or schools of art in the twentieth century. A work of art does not exist in a vacuum. If you come to understand something of how the different "isms" began, when and in what part of the world they first appeared and how they relate to one another, you'll begin to look at any given work in its historical context, and thereby come to appreciate the story it tells about changes in the culture of humankind.

3

FIGURATIVE ART

olumes have been written on the history of art and its various movements by scholars and art historians. I am neither. I like to think of this book as a journal of my thirty years' experience in the art business, first as a self-taught student, later as director of a department store gallery and finally as a private art dealer. Using what I have learned, I'll attempt to provide a simple road map for you to follow on your own odyssey into the delightful world of art.

I am fascinated by books about the intimate lives of artists, their times, their conversations and the cultural ambience in which they lived. I have already mentioned James Mellows's *The Charmed Circle: Gertrude Stein and Company*, a delightful account of the famous writer/collector and her brilliant friends during the twenties in Paris. Reading it, I felt I was there listening to Picasso, Matisse, Sherwood Anderson and

Hemingway, while Alice B. Toklas served us coffee. I felt I was in such magical company that my own world held no interest for me until I finished the book. In the bibliography I will list other books like Mellows's which will make you feel a part of an artist's inner circle, as well as some of the great critical works on modern and twentieth-century art, so that you can continue your education, if you're so inclined.

In general, people who are just beginning to look at art seriously are drawn to recognizable images: landscapes, the human face and form, buildings, still-life's. The familiar is always more comfortable than the unknown. When van Gogh paints a sunflower, no matter how he intensifies its color to create a mood, we recognize it as a sunflower. Modigliani may elongate a woman's face and body, but she remains a woman. A Picasso bull may have both eyes on the same side, but it's unmistakably a bull. Any picture or sculpture with an identifiable shape, figure or object in it, no matter how greatly transformed by the artist's personal vision, is a *figurative* or *objective* work of art

By contrast, in a *nonobjective* work, although the artist may have begun with a landscape or a human figure in mind, he or she has variously simplified or distorted the subject matter according to an inner vision—Cubist paintings, for example, are *nonobjective*, but the careful viewer will always be able to discern the fragmented lines of a guitar, a violin, a woman's profile, a vase of flowers. A strict *abstract* artist abandons the literal image altogether, and works in terms of pure forms of color and shape, arranged in patterns which might be said to convey his *idea* of the given image and his *feelings* about it.

He is intentionally altering reality to the point where we can no longer recognize it.

But how can an artist look at an actual landscape, say, and then render it without the trees, hills, clouds and so forth that *make* it a landscape? A little experiment may give you an idea of the process. Next time you are out in the country, close your eyes *tightly* for a few seconds and then open them quickly to take in your surroundings. In the split second before your eyes refocus, you won't see the details of the landscape as recognizable objects. The hills and trees will appear, instead, as masses of color and intermingled shapes—abstract rectangles, ovals and irregular patterns. After that instant, when your eyes are back in focus, the large dark mass in the foreground will turn out to be a cow, the skinny tall green form, a tree coming into leaf, the red oblong, the side of a barn. But in the fleeting instant before recognition kicks in, you'll have experienced something of the way the abstract artist has trained himself to see. He is pulling up the *essence* of the scene.

Try another seeing experiment. Pluck a leaf from a tree and study it closely. At first glance it just looks green—but further study reveals many different shades of green, and other colors as well. The stem may be brown, the veins purplish, the surface between them a variety of blues, yellows and even pinks within the dominant green. Your immediate perception of the "green" leaf has been changed by your intense scrutiny. Nonfigurative artists work from just such altered ways of seeing: a leaf, to them, is never simply green.

Abstract artists of another category choose not to deal with reality at all. They have reduced their visual expressions to geometric or irregular arrangements of color and line without any reference to specific objects.

I find that people who prefer abstract to figurative art tend to have a strong affinity for pure pattern and design and an instinctive appreciation of architectural forms. But preference for one style or the other doesn't matter. What is important is to understand *why* you like *what* you like, and to learn exactly what it is you are looking at. As I said above, no work of art exists in a vacuum: from the beginning of history artists, consciously or not, have mirrored their societies. In earlier centuries, artists depended upon patronage. When they executed portraits of noblemen and their families, they were expected to flatter their patrons. But great artists managed to penetrate beneath the flattering conventions of portraiture to reveal the truth about their societies. Look into the eyes of an arrogant lord in all his finery, as portrayed by Velázquez or Goya. In those eyes we recognize the cruelty of the man and his supreme satisfaction in the power he wields.

I've used an example from a period outside the scope of this book to underline the point that artists have always been simultaneously the product of their cultures and the critics of these very cultures, at once insiders and outsiders. Many groups of artists who painted in the same venue adopted manifestoes proclaiming their rebellion against the old values of their cultures. You will see that each movement arose in reaction to a specific cultural situation. But before going on, I want to emphasize that my interpretations are very personal, based on my experience. I certainly don't pretend that my understanding of a given movement's purpose is that of the artists who created it. Art movements and schools, like individual paintings and sculpture, should ultimately be defined by the individual viewer. There is no reason for you to see any work of art, or define any "ism," exactly as I do. Question authority, as the saying goes. My responses reflect my way of seeing: so should yours. In time, as your knowledge and understanding widen and deepen, you'll come up with your own way of understanding the various schools of art.

In the following pages I'll present a series of capsule descriptions of the more widely known figurative schools of art, reserving the abstract movements for the next chapter.

1: IMPRESSIONISM

Although it began in the latter part of the nineteenth century, Impressionism produced the first modern art. The movement represented a distinct break with the traditional figurative mode which had dominated European art history. Its eventual acceptance opened the way for the constant experimentation and innovation which characterize twentieth-century art.

Impressionism developed slowly through the 1860s, before erupting stunningly upon the Parisian cultural scene in 1874. The explosion was caused by young "radical" artists—Manet, Pissarro, Renoir, Degas, Morisot, Sisley, Guillamin and Cézanne. Year after year their experimental new work had been turned down by the inflexible jury which selected paintings for the French Academy's annual Grand Salon exhibition. But in 1874 they decided to mount their own exhibition, on April 15—one month *before* the Grand Salon. They had no money to rent a space, but fortunately the dealer Paul Durand Ruel, one of their first champions, was moving out of his gallery and let them have the rooms for free. The audacity of the group of young artists in scheduling their show in a fashionable section of Paris a month before the official Academy exhibition brought down the wrath of the art establishment.

Curiosity and a one-franc admission charge brought critics and art connoisseurs in to see what this aberration was all about. The reaction was instantaneous, and furious. The critics wrote pages and pages calling the work an affront to the civilized tradition of art, executed by untrained and talentless Bohemians. Paris's most influential newspaper, *Le Soir*, referred to the painters as lunatics in an asylum. Its critic went on to say that true art was a "decoration of beauty, not this disgusting rubbish."

Louis Leroy, writing for another newspaper, *Charivari*, ridiculed the exhibition, labeling it derisively the "Salon des Refusés," for the fact that all the work, except a painting by Monet, had been refused by the official Salon. He went on to say, with equal contempt, that the painters weren't painting from Nature, but from their impression of Nature. His term of derision was, in fact, an accurate description of what the artists were trying to do: they painted their subjective impressions of the natural world. With ironic glee they embraced Leroy's intended insult and proclaimed themselves Impressionists.

The public took up the critics' cudgels enthusiastically. There were violent demonstrations and near-riots on the street where the *Salon des Refusés* was held. Not one picture was sold.

The fury of the reaction may be understood in part when we remember that in the mid-nineteenth century Parisians took the art of the academicians seriously. Of course radio, movies and television didn't exist, and even photography was in its infancy. Art, music, drama and literature made up the media of the period, and cultural revolutions took place in salons, concert halls, galleries and academies of art. All controversial subjects were hotly debated daily in the newspapers. Prior to Impressionism, French art had been ruled absolutely by the officially sanctioned academies, from the dozens of small teaching studios to the lordly French Academy itself, a government body which dictated precisely what was art and what wasn't. An attack on the Academy's orthodoxy represented, to the average Frenchman, an attack on France itself.

The Neo-Classical painter Ingres represented perfection in the eyes of the Academy. His idealized nudes, done to marble perfection in cool hues, were decorative enough, despite the fact that the women were technically naked, to appeal both to the upper classes and to the rising bourgeoisie. Ingres's rigid rules of technique were followed slavishly in the teaching studios. A model was posed before the students, and a perfectly executed, line-for-line, shadow-for-shadow, highlight-for-highlight copy of the model was demanded. Only after the exact rendering passed the Master's inspection was the student artist free to fill in the rest of the picture. Color was irrelevant: only the line was important. John Rewald remarks in *The History of Impressionism* that according to the leading Academic teachers and critics of the 1870s, Renoir "succumbed to the vice of color."

At the Grand Salon each year, canvases and sculptures by established Academicians predominated, but work by a few new artists was featured as well. The Academy Salon was absolutely crucial to the young artists who flocked to Paris every year to enroll in the various ateliers: if their work was accepted by the Salon, their futures were virtually assured.

Although the academic followers of Ingres made preliminary sketches out of doors, they did their finished paintings exclusively in studios where the light could be controlled. The Impressionists, by contrast, took all their equipment—sketch pads, easels, canvases, paints and brushes—outside, where the weather could alter the landscape in a second. With every hour the light changed, and the artists learned to work quickly. They weren't painting the actual landscape as such, but the way the light played upon the scene. For example, Monet, in his "Waterlilies" series, was not concerned with an exact rendering of the plants themselves or the details of the pond in which they floated, but with the light and shadow that shifted across the flowers and the water from moment to moment. He also concentrated on capturing the changing light, from dawn to dusk and from season to season, in his "Haystacks" sequence and in the number of paintings he made of Rouen Cathedral.

Similarly, Degas painted ballet dancers in a practice studio, depicting them in the same poses, but letting the light coming through the window at different times of day change the mood of the canvases. He also caught the effect of artificial light by showing his ballerinas onstage, lit from below by gas footlights, which made his subjects appear to float like supernatural beings. Light was the object of the Impressionists' passionate curiosity.

A few years ago I went to an exhibition of Impressionists at the Petit Palais in Paris. Hanging side by side were a Monet and a Renoir. Both paintings presented the same scene, at the same time of day: a group of people in a rowboat on a lake. The two painters had gone to the lake together, and had set up their easels side by side. What was striking to me was how different the paintings were: each artist expressed his individual vision within the Impressionistic style. The Renoir had a misty, hazy atmosphere, while the reflected lights and shadows of the Monet were stronger and the scene more clearly defined. Two artists of the same school, with the same subject before them—yet each with his own powerful interpretation.

In 1876 the Impressionists were again turned down by the Grand Salon. Paul Durand Ruel lent them his new gallery for a second show, simply called *Exposition de Peinture*. This

Pierre-Auguste Renoir: *Le Petit Peintre,*
Sanguine and white chalk, circa 1905, 22¾ × 17¾"
Courtesy of: Mr. and Mrs. Charles Perrin, Connecticut

time around a few critics defended the work. But an important critic named Wolf wrote maliciously, "Five or six lunatics and one woman (Berthe Morisot), besotted with ambition, have gathered to show this undefendable work." The second show was also a failure. It wasn't until 1882, eight years after the first exhibition, that an Impressionist show was accepted by the critics and the public, and the artists actually sold their work. Ironically, by that time the original Impressionists who had fought for their collective vision for so long were already beginning to split up and go their separate ways, growing artistically and exploring new techniques.

The Impressionists brought to art a radical new way of seeing: an outdoor vision of nature bathed in light and color. Their startling perception was considered inexcusably alien at first. Only the passage of time made it familiar, something people could finally understand and come to love. Impressionism today is as "safe" a style as Ingres's Neo-Classicism was to the people of the 1870s. It's important to remember how daringly it challenged the status quo in art when it first appeared.

2: POST-IMPRESSIONISM

Post-Impressionism arrived no more than two years after Impressionism reached its height. Cézanne, a giant in the history of art, withdrew from the tightly knit Impressionist circle in 1878. He, Seurat, Gauguin, van Gogh and Bonnard, all of whom had begun as Impressionists, were the most important artists who split from the main movement. Each of them decided that Impressionism, with its narrow focus upon landscape and the human figure, was limiting. They were more interested in exploring color and structure, and unlike the Impressionists, for the most part they worked alone. Although they retained the colors—the palette, to use the technical term—of Impressionism, they abandoned the hazy wash of light for stronger and purer tones.

Paul Gauguin, for instance, painted vibrant tropical scenes in the vivid colors of Tahiti, where he did his most famous work. Henri de Toulouse-Lautrec used techniques borrowed from graphic art, highly concentrated blocks of color arranged two-dimensionally on a neutral background: though he executed some magnificent paintings, he is best known for his splendid posters and prints depicting the prostitutes in the brothels of Paris and the dancers and singers in cabarets like the famous Moulin Rouge.

Van Gogh left Paris and Impressionism behind and settled in the south of France, where he fell in love with its intense, almost blinding light. He was subject to periodic bouts of mental illness which confined him to various asylums (today he is considered to have been a manic-depressive—and contrary to romantic myth, he did not, *could* not paint during his attacks of madness, as his letters to his brother Theo specifically point out). In his lucid periods, however, he turned out an astounding number of magnificent paintings which sought to capture that furious light. In his urgency, he often applied thick gouts of pigment directly to the canvas with a palette knife—a technique very different from the Impressionists' lightness and subtlety.

The Post-Impressionists did not completely lose the Impressionist fascination with landscape and the human figure, but they were looking for more than the play of light and the nuances of color in their subjects. They attempted to break through color and light to find the basic structures of nature. Cézanne, in his mature work, broke down landscape into pure blocks and planes, a technique which formed the basis for Cubism, a later movement which would take Cézanne's

Henri de Toulouse-Lautrec: *Street Acquaintances*,
Oil on board, circa 1889, 50.2 × 38.1 cm
Courtesy of: Private Collection, New York

concern with the essential architecture of natural objects even further.

When you look at a Cézanne or a Gauguin, then at a Pissarro or a Renoir, you will recognize immediately the Post-Impressionists' concern with structure and concentration upon individual elements, and their more forceful use of pure pigment: the chief factors which differentiate Post-Impressionism from its parent movement.

At the time when the French Impressionists had finally won some acceptance, American artists were still working in the academic tradition. But some American painters who had heard of the exciting experiment moved to Paris in the 1870s and 1880s. Among these expatriates were James MacNeil Whistler, Mary Cassatt and Kenneth Frazier. They studied and worked side by side with French Impressionists and Post-Impressionists, and their work eventually reached the United States, where a new generation of American painters eagerly embraced it. In addition to the painters mentioned above, Childe Hassam, George Innes and Maurice Prendergast were among the notable American Impressionists.

Their imagery, although done in the Impressionistic style, has a distinctly American quality which lies chiefly in the choice of deeper, earthier, rawer colors, and a preference for stronger delineation compared to the French school's hazy atmospherics. American Impressionism, which lasted into the first decade of the twentieth century, is certainly important in the history of American art, but it doesn't have the worldwide significance of the original French Impressionist movement.

Edgar Degas: *Two Studies of Mary Cassatt*,
Pastel, circa 1879, 47.8 × 63 cm
Courtesy of: Private Collection, New York

Paul Cézanne: *Still Life*,
Oil on canvas, circa 1830, 18 × 14½"
Courtesy of: Private Collection, New York

3: POINTILLISM

Pointillism was not, strictly speaking, a movement unto itself, but rather a style within the Post-Impressionist school. It was at its zenith for only two years, between 1885 and 1887. The Pointillists took an approach to light and color that was similar to that of the Impressionists, but they executed their paintings in dots and points of pigment, to break down seemingly solid colors into the subtle elements that made it up. In a Pointillist painting of a blue lake, for example, there might be an area of pink dots, because to the artist's eye the light on that part of the lake shifted into the red end of the spectrum. When you see such a painting from a distance, the pink dots blend with dots of other colors—some of them even blue—to form a single color, the individual dots becoming invisible, and the lake looking as if it's been painted in large, sweeping brush strokes. As you move closer, you'll see the dominant blue breaking up into the thousands of tiny dots— blue, pink, yellow, green, red and white—which make it up, until at close range the image of the lake disappears altogether. Step back again, and as if by magic the painting returns to an unbroken expanse of blue water in sunlight.

The Pointillists' concern was the breaking down of light itself, and their astonishing paintings were done painstakingly, dot by dot. Anyone who knows Stephen Sondheim's musical play *Sunday in the Park with George*, based on the career and work of the Pointillist Georges Seurat, will recall the central character complaining in song about how difficult and tedious—yet immensely exciting—the technique was.

Seurat was the most extraordinary artist of the Pointillist school. The eminent Impressionist Pissarro was so impressed by Seurat's exacting experiments that in later years he tried his own hand at Pointillism, with marked success. Some other skillful Pointillists were Henri Edmond Cross, Sisley and Signac. But it was a difficult style, and most painters simply couldn't make it work. Recently I visited the Clark Museum in Williamstown, Massachusetts, where I found a charming Pointillist painting by Pissarro, hanging with three or four by another Pointillist whose work looked crude by comparison. How could I tell? As I mentioned earlier, look and look, and eventually you will feel through your eyes what is good and what is not.

But no other Pointillist compares with Seurat, who invented the style. His scientific breakdown of the Impressionists' romantic haze of colors into their constituent dots was similar to what Cézanne and the other Post-Impressionists were doing when they brought out the structural forms underlying their scenes. Seurat's drawings in black and white are remarkable. Seen up close, they appear to be nothing but tiny commas of charcoal on white paper. Move back, and just as with his paintings, the commas blend into recognizable forms with depth and perspective.

4: FAUVISM

Seurat's brilliant analysis of the structure of color had a tremendous influence on Matisse and others who formed the Fauve movement a few years later. Fauvism, like Pointillism, was part of the general Post-Impressionist school. Its heyday was a short period at the turn of the century, between 1905 and 1907. The Fauves used pure, brilliant color, often applied directly to the canvas from the tube of paint. The Fauves shared the Impressionists' passion for landscapes, still-life's and the human figure, but their work was nothing like their forerunners' gentle play of light and color. Their canvases assaulted the eye with strong, violent hues.

Fauve, in French, means "Wild Beast," and like "Impressionist," it was originally a term of derision applied to the painters by shocked critics. Taking chances, challenging the status quo, pushing *beyond*, have always been part of the genuine artist's task, and the Fauves were delighted to be thought dangerous animals who used paintbrushes as if they were teeth and claws.

Henri Matisse was the leading Fauve. He worked each area of his canvas as a positive value, considering the empty spaces of equal value with the objects in the painting. During his Fauve period (for he went on to other styles), Matisse reveled in pure pigment, and the blocks of solid color surrounding his subjects—people, still-life arrangements and so forth—are as important to his designs as the subjects themselves. Color was his first concern, line far less important.

As mentioned, Fauvism took its inspiration from the Pointillist deconstruction of color, though its technique was quite different. Thus a Fauve scene at dusk might include a pink cow or a blue cloud, because the setting sun cast a rose-blue glow on the natural landscape. For artists like Matisse, Fauvism was a transitional style, abandoned after only a couple of years. But Derain and Vlaminck continued to paint Fauvist canvases for six or seven years, and in my view, they did their most important work during that period.

5: EXPRESSIONISM

The Fauves' concentration upon the equal weight of empty, "negative" space and subject matter found a formal structure in Expressionism. As we've seen, the Impressionists painted the external effects of light and color upon their subjects. By contrast, the Expressionists used strong colors and powerful, often distorted, shapes to express the way they *felt* about their subjects. If Impressionism was ultimately an *objective* way of seeing, with the painter working out-of-doors to convey, swiftly and surely, the exact effect of light upon landscape, Expressionism was intensely *subjective*, a method of expressing the painter's emotions about his subjects.

Compare Monet's waterlilies to flower paintings by the Expressionist Emil Nolde. Monet's flowers almost dissolve into gentle nuances of light and shadow. In Nolde's canvases the bold flower forms, rendered in brilliant, dense colors, predominate.

The leading Expressionist artists at the beginning of the movement were Germans: Nolde, Beckmann, Feininger, Heckel and Kirshner, along with the brilliant Norwegian Edvard Munch. Originating in Dresden in 1905, this group was collectively known as *Die Brücke*, "The Bridge." The Germans went on to dominate Expressionism into the early 1930s. Obsessed with the decadence of German society after the First World War, they pictured their world in dark and murky colors, using thick brush strokes and a heavy application of the palette knife. They exaggerated and distorted the human figure, using crude, jagged lines to suggest the brutality and violence, the emotional and moral bankruptcy of German life.

During the same period Expressionism cropped up in Austria as well. Like the Germans, the Austrian Expressionists were concerned with the flaws in their own morally impoverished society. But the Austrian world was more formal, mannered and hypocritical, and Austrian artists reflected the difference by a more decorative approach which involved lighter and more delicate techniques. The best-known Austrian Expressionists—Schiele, Klimt and Kokoschka—are devastating in their sardonic portrayals of the artificial society in which they lived.

Before World War I, there had been a group of Expressionists known as *Der Blaue Reiter* ("The Blue Rider"), but they were dispersed by the outbreak of the war. The group included two Russians, Kandinsky (who eventually pioneered Abstract Expressionism) and Jawlensky. Other members of *Der Blaue Reiter* were the Germans Franz Marc, August Macke and Gabrielle Münter, and the Swiss, Paul Klee. With their blue horses and pink cows, *Der Blaue Reiter* showed the strong influence of the French Fauves.

Artists like Georg Grosz and Max Beckmann saw Expressionism through to the end. They featured stark depictions of the victims of the First World War, and later they used deliberately crude, brutal imagery to illustrate the corrupt and disillusioned society of pre-Hitler Germany. When the Nazis came to power, Expressionism was banned as "degenerate art," and its exhibition was forbidden. The raw emotions of Expressionism were echoed in the Social Realist School of America's Great Depression.

6: CUBISM

Cubism, the most radical movement in modern art, changed forever the way a painting is executed and perceived. Though it has abstract elements, Cubism is fundamentally figurative: it deals with real objects. In simplified terms, the Cubists took the flat planes of a chair, a human face or figure, a musical instrument, a still-life, etc., and rearranged them in geometric blocks or cubes in paint or collage to allow us to see the objects from more than one angle.

When we think of Cubism, we must think first of Pablo

Max Beckmann: *Grosses Selbstbildnis* (Large Self-Portrait),
Drypoint, 1919, 9½ × 7¾"
Courtesy of: Alice Adam Ltd., Chicago

Georg Grosz: *Die Abfahrt*,
Ink drawing, 1926, 24½ × 18¾"
Courtesy of: Mrs. Hanny Multer, New York
© 1997 Estate of George Grosz/Licensed by VAGA, New York, NY.

Picasso and Georges Braque. But long before these painters, there were African sculptors who simplified the human form to blocks and planes. And in the Italian Renaissance, Piero della Francesca, among others, explored the structure of cubed planes in altered perspective. Cézanne was the immediate forerunner of the Cubist movement: from his beginnings he always looked for the inner structure in his landscapes, nature's essential building blocks.

Around 1905 Picasso and Braque, influenced by Cézanne and by African sculpture recently exhibited in Paris, began to explore the breaking up of surface appearances, rearranging reality as most people saw it. Cubism was a decidedly intellectual exercise in the history of art. Be that as it may, after Cubism was born, one could no longer look at art pictorially, simply admiring a painter's approach to a recognizable image. Picasso and Braque fractured their subjects and, to a far greater extent than Cézanne, reduced them to abstract forms. But Picasso and Braque never abandoned real objects altogether: however fractured and scattered their images may be, you can always see the guitar, the vase of flowers, the human face, forming the foundations of their Cubist experiments.

In 1907, at the age of twenty-six, Picasso executed his famous *Les Demoiselles d'Avignon*, a grouping of nude women, distorted by the African masks some of them wear, and by the manipulation of planar surfaces he had picked up from Cézanne and the other Post-Impressionists. Picasso's colleague Georges Braque executed the first purely Cubist painting. Braque was actually more of an abstract painter than Picasso, but during the brief time the two shared a studio, the "Analytical Cubist" paintings they produced are hard to distinguish. In later years Picasso abandoned the severe fracturing and planar shifting of Analytical Cubism and the

Pablo Picasso: *Le Pont Neuf*,
Oil on canvas, 1911, 33 × 24 cm
Courtesy of: Private Collection, Switzerland
© 1997 Estate of Pablo Picasso/Artists Rights Society (ARS), New York.

limited brown-black-gray palette to reintroduce instantly recognizable images in his paintings. Braque, though he never entirely abandoned the real-world subjects he painted, followed the fragmenting progress throughout his career. He, more than Picasso, was a forerunner of the pure Abstract movement.

The artistic climate in Paris had changed since the early struggles of the Impressionists, and in 1911 Cubism was formally recognized as a movement in Paris, at the Salon des Indépendents and the Salon d'Automne. In 1913 the Armory Show in New York City featured Cubism—Picassos and Braques, Marcel Duchamps's famous *Nude Descending a Staircase*—alongside gritty realistic pictures by the American "Ashcan School." Public reaction to Cubism was as savage as that which had greeted the Impressionists in their first exhibition decades before.

But Cubism was a fact. The pioneers, Picasso and Braque, joined by Juan Gris, influenced many artists who came after them, notably Fernand Léger and Henri Laurens, and many others who used the technique more decoratively than seriously.

By 1915 the Dutch artist Piet Mondrian and the Russians Kasimir Malevich and Vasily Kandinsky, strongly influenced by Cubism, had taken a step into pure abstraction which shocked even their contemporaries. Picasso never entirely abandoned Cubism's concern with showing all sides and aspects of his subjects, as if the flat plane of the canvas were a motion-picture screen. But formal Cubism faded by the 1920s.

7: DADA

Dada, born in Zurich, Switzerland, in the year 1915, was actually an *anti*-art movement, a revolt against pretentious aesthetic theories and bourgeois over-intellectualizing, not only in art, but in literature and politics as well. The Dadaists took ordinary objects out of context and presented them as works of art—one thinks of Marcel Duchamps's famous fur-lined toilet seat. The movement was strongly political, mocking the nationalism of its period and ridiculing the slogans and propaganda which urged young men to march off to war and die for their countries. Tristan Tzara, known better as a poet than an artist, was a key figure in Dada, although in keeping with the anti-rhetorical spirit of the movement he was careful never to define "Dada" in his writings.

Over the years I've heard many self-styled authorities trying to explain the meaning of the word. A while ago I attended a party at an art dealer's house, and was introduced to Dr. Richard Huelsenbach, then in his eighties. Dr. Huelsenbach, a writer who later became a psychiatrist here in the States, had been a member of the original Dada group in Zurich. I asked him what Dada meant.

"Nothing at all," he said. "We used it to undercut the fancy lingo used by the pretentious bourgeoisie. When they tried to intellectualize and used pompous rhetoric to talk about Life and Art, we'd just answer, 'Da da da da da . . .'— baby noises to throw their infantile pronouncements back at them."

Along with the Frenchman Duchamps, the artists identified with Dada are the Swiss sculptor Hans Arp, Picabia, Hans Richter and the man who became the "father of Surrealism," Max Ernst. As mentioned, Dada involved literature—poetry and socio-political writing—at least as much as art. André Breton and Tristan Tzara were Dada's most important writers, mocking the conventional styles of their period by exaggerating them to absurdity.

8: SURREALISM

It is easy to see how Surrealism evolved from the wild and energetic Dadaist writers and artists. In the small but important movement, which arose in Europe during the twenties and thirties, Surrealists took the grand oratory of the Dada writers and the mock grandeur of Dada artists, which had already presented a vision of the world that was larger than life, and pushed them to their logical—or sublimely illogical—extreme. *"Sureat"* in French literally means "above real," and to give concrete expression to the concept, the artists turned to the human subconscious, drawing upon the researches of Sigmund Freud, whose psychoanalytic writing was beginning to be widely accepted during the period. Surrealists depict the images and scenes we see in our dreams, strangely charged symbols like Salvador Dalí's dripping clocks and watches, Magritte's enigmatic man in the bowler hat or his immense boulders eerily suspended in midair, Delvaux's elongated women grouped beneath the moon in a mysterious nether world, or Matta's landscapes apparently made up of machine-fragments from another planet. Surrealism waned after the Second World War, but it continued to influence the later work of Hans Bellmer, Alexander Calder, Paul Klee and Joan Miró.

René Magritte: *Le ciel passe en l'air,*
Oil on canvas, circa 1923–29, 50 × 65 cm
Courtesy of: Private Collection, Switzerland
© 1997 C. Herscovici, Brussels/Artists Rights Society (ARS), New York.

9: SOCIAL REALISM

Social Realism is predominately an American art movement, although as we have seen it derives from aspects of German Expressionism. The Social Realist is moved by the harsh conditions of his society and the alienation of the individual within it. The movement is specifically identified with the Depression of the 1930s. A few powerful examples express the essence of the school.

Most of us know Edward Hopper's brooding *Night Cafe* through poster or postcard reproductions, even if we've never seen the original canvas: it is one of the most famous images of the Depression. A man in work clothes, probably out of a job, sits alone in an all-night diner with a cup of coffee, ignored by the counterman. We see him through a harshly lit window and forcefully feel his hopelessness and desolation.

Another powerful painting of this school is Ben Shahn's *The Passion of Sacco and Vanzetti*. It depicts the violent, angry mood of a desperate people venting their misery and frustration upon two immigrant laborers who were put to death on questionable charges of anarchism and treason.

Jack Levine's *The Gangster's Funeral* evokes the Prohibition period, when gangsterism—legal and illegal—threatened to take over the United States. Levine's brutal armed thugs are icons of social commentary.

Many Social Realist works, with their strong, simplified lines and blunt "messages," will remind you of the German Expressionist technique. The savage, overfed faces of Georg Grosz's pre-Hitler burghers are the same faces we see among the thuggish mourners in the Levine painting. The social statement of the work is at least as important to the Social Realist as its aesthetic values.

10: POP ART

There was no major figurative art movement after the schools of Surrealism and Social Realism until Pop emerged in the early sixties (the major movements from the end of World War II through the fifties were *nonfigurative*, and we'll cover them in the next chapter). Pop Art is pure American. Claes Oldenburg, Andy Warhol and Roy Lichtenstein portrayed American consumer society blatantly and outrageously, using its own advertising imagery and mass-market graphic designs to point out the public's utter lack of discrimination in accepting with infantile greed whatever it is fed by the media.

Oldenburg invented the "soft sculpture"—collapsed drums, stuffed plastic hamburgers, showcases of pies and cakes, musical instruments and other common objects rendered in cloth and other soft materials. Mocking grandiose corporate architecture, he also drew up plans for skyscraper-high sculptures of totally banal items—a clothespin the size of the Statue of Liberty, for example, or a gargantuan toilet-tank float to be moored in the Thames River in London.

Warhol glorified the Campbell's Soup can and was the creator of endless serial portraits of such popular icons as Marilyn Monroe and Mao Zedong, oversized silkscreen renditions taken from photographs and colorized. He also executed an explosive, outsized rendering of an electric chair, done in simplified, cartoonlike lines as it might have appeared on a billboard, thereby forcing the viewer to confront the hideous banality of its details.

In the early to mid-sixties, Roy Lichtenstein took his inspiration directly from actual comic books and newspaper cartoons, which he enlarged on his painted canvases right down to the dots of the original printing process. His men

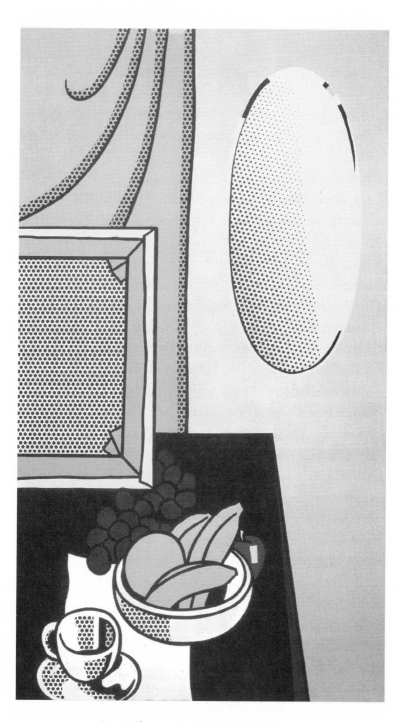

Roy Lichtenstein: *Still Life with Mirror,*
Oil and magna on canvas, 1972, 96 × 54"
Courtesy of: James Goodman Gallery, New York

were two-dimensional, their features too regularly handsome to be lifelike; his women similarly cartoonlike, with perfectly symmetrical features and stylized swoops of blonde or blue-black hair. The captions to these canvases were drawn from soap operas, war comics and advertising illustrations: "Darling, tell me the truth, the honest truth, did you prefer the other toothpaste?" says one vapid blonde. A dark-haired girl who seems to be drowning says, "I'd rather sink than ask Brad for help!" Lichtenstein's characters are really nothing but commercial products: with his fellow Pop Artists, he is presenting the emptiness of a society dominated by hype and cliché. Pop technique is visually flat, deliberately void of any emotional quality. Warhol's soup can with its colorful label is saying, "I'm a catchy can, but there's no soup inside—and none in your society, either." It's interesting to note that the Europeans, long scornful of American consumerism, latched on to Pop before the American public accepted it, even though it was our invention.

Pop puzzles people. I am constantly asked what the soup cans, squashy plastic hamburgers, giant comic strips and so on are all about. Judge for yourself: as usual throughout this book, I've given you my own opinions of the Pop Artists' intentions. You may disagree, and that's fine.

11: SUPER REALISM

Just as Dadaism influenced Pop, Pop influenced Super Realism, which emerged in the early 1970s. To me the work that typifies the movement is Richard Estes's *The Gasoline Station*. The painting is presented with such photographic precision that at first glance you aren't sure if you are looking at a picture of a gas station, or seeing an actual one through a window. But the color and lines, the light and volume are somehow *too* real, more vivid than a photograph, more lifelike than life. This is reality taken to the very edge of waking perception. Estes, Chuck Close and Alfred Leslie copy ordinary American scenes with such excruciatingly meticulous exactitude (I think particularly of Leslie's detailed and detached scene of an accident) that the effects are disturbing. There are no human feelings in these paintings—and, often, no humans. In Estes's picture of a Woolworth's store, the items for sale are presented in perfect rows on the counters, but there is not a single human figure present. Like the Pop Artists, Super Realists are commenting on the sterility of a consumer-driven society which places more value upon things than people. But where the Pop Artists included images, however ironically cartoonish, of men and women, the later school bypasses human life altogether. In the presence of a Super Realist canvas we feel diminished, rendered almost invisible in a world where lifeless things have taken over.

There was no identifiable school or movement in the eighties. It was a decade of frenzied greed for artists and galleries, a time for bad artists as well as good ones to make hay while the sun shone. There was a wealth of new collectors, the majority of whom had no idea of the difference between fine art and superficial rubbish. The price was everything: the more expensive, the greater the art must be, so bid high.

Those who felt the need to categorize artists invented the term Neo-Expressionist for a group of German painters, including Baselitz, Anselm Kiefer and Immendorf, who were glorified during the eighties. There were also many mediocre artists during the period that were elevated to *great*, and even the museums bought into the hype. Some of the artists who

Robert Cottingham: *An American Alphabet,*
Oil on canvas, 1994–96, 126 × 300 " (10.5 × 25 feet)
Courtesy of: Forum Gallery, New York

made it big during the height of the hype (by big, I mean their work sold in the high hundred-thousands) were David Salle, Eric Fischl, Julian Schnabel and Donald Sultan. Their dealers promoted them to the skies, and an unlearned public was happy to pay ridiculous prices for a "new" discovery. With demand outstripping supply during the decade, it sometimes seemed that every kid who could hold a paintbrush was considered a master. . . .

Today I rarely see work by any of the above-named artists come up for sale at auction. It's a more serious, more sober time, and there is considerable fear that many of the artists whose name was on every neophyte collector's tongue in the eighties either won't sell at all, or will sell far lower than their original prices. Collectors and dealers who bought these artists during the boom are keeping their works hidden, hoping that the crazy market will come back. Which is doubtful, in my opinion.

I am optimistic about the nineties. I'm seeing serious and solid work by young artists, and new collectors are buying their pieces for all the right reasons, and at realistic prices. I am also seeing the work of some very fine, experienced artists, men and women who have quietly honed their talents and refined their visions even though they've been passed over by the art establishment for many years, finally coming into their own and receiving the recognition they deserve, as well as artists not recognized in their lifetimes surfacing to more knowledgeable collectors.

It should be noted that there are many artists who use styles and techniques taken from any and all of the "isms" cited, passing through several movements as transitional stages in the development of their individual visions. The so-called School of Paris, for example, was not a movement at all, but a group of very different artists who merely happened to work in the same city at roughly the same time. Arman, Soulage, Modigliani, Giacometti and Dubuffet could not be more individual in their approaches to art: they do not make up a unified group. Not every artist can be safely stuck into a pigeonhole. . . .

4

ABSTRACT ART

1: EUROPEAN BEGINNINGS AND THE ARMORY SHOW

bstract Art is not simple to define. There are no familiar guidelines—no recognizable landscapes, human figures, picnics in the grass, no scenes to evoke long-forgotten memories. Robert Motherwell, an American Abstract Artist, describes abstractness as reality *felt*, rather than *seen*, and suggests that we viewers, in turn, allow ourselves to respond to whatever we are feeling as we stand before an abstract canvas or sculpture. The unsophisticated eye sees random patchworks of color, or lines that seem to lead nowhere. At first glance, we have no idea where the artist is coming from.

As with figurative art, some understanding of the society in which Abstract Artists lived, and the culture which spawned their philosophies, will deepen your understanding and appreciation of their work. I'm not saying you *have* to like Non-Figurative Art. But with some background, you'll know better why you respond to it (or don't). All original works of art begin, of course, in the head of the creator, whether he or she is a visual artist, a writer or a musician. First comes a concept, an idea, a reflection, a philosophy: the artist's reaction to his or her society, which strives to change, or at least transcend, the strictures of that society. Abstract art is not an intellectual exercise.

When I was first introduced to Abstract, Non-Objective, Constructivist Art—the terms were interchangeable, it held no interest for me. I saw nothing but masses of color, random squares and black lines. I felt as if I had entered a foreign land where I didn't speak the language or understand the customs. In fact I wasn't certain at all that the stuff wasn't fake. The painters, I thought, probably couldn't draw a human form or a real field of wheat.

Since then I have learned that *all* of the Non-Objective Artists began by painting traditional, figurative paintings. Franz Kline's Depression-Era study of ex-servicemen is as realistic a canvas as one might find. Jackson Pollock's early paintings of regional America were precisely figurative in execution. Today we think mostly of the later work of the Dutch artist Piet Mondrian, with its rectangular grids in black, white and the primary colors; yet his early paintings, drawn from a tradition of Dutch realism that reaches back to Rembrandt and Vermeer, are beautiful. If you are ever fortunate enough to view a single, ethereal flower by the young

Mondrian, it will make you catch your breath with awe at his vision and skill.

The same solid grounding in traditional drawing and painting applies to all the recognized Abstractionists. Each of them began with the basics and reached a point where realistic depiction of the natural world no longer satisfied his creative instincts. Only then did he venture into works of pure abstraction. I'm sure you have heard, as I have, a parent confronted by a Joan Miró line drawing or a Pollock "drip" canvas, declaring, "Why, my six-year-old son can do that!" He can't. He lacks the training, the long immersion in technique, and the mature philosophy which, combined, make even the wildest, most radical Abstract painting ultimately "readable." At most, if the six-year-old is something of a child prodigy, he might *copy* a Mondrian square, line for line, or drip everything in his paintbox onto the paper in the manner of Jackson Pollock. But his efforts will be as lifeless as those of the Sunday painters and students who set up their easels at the Louvre in Paris to copy the *Mona Lisa*. Even the most painstaking copies lack the thought, the original concept, the lively impulse of their originals—which is one reason a trained eye can spot a deliberately faked Pollock as easily as a faked Leonardo. I don't mean to dismiss the paintings and drawings of children: they are often fresh and powerful. But it's apples and oranges to compare a six-year-old's energetic splashings to the work of a mature artist working from everything she or he has learned over decades of experimentation and practice. Meanwhile, stick the child's pictures on the refrigerator door and enjoy them.

Abstract Art, in the broadest sense of the term, came out of Russia. Vasily Kandinsky, in his autobiography *Der Rückblick*, published in Germany, remembers a moment of revelation which happened in 1908. One day at dusk he entered his studio and saw a strange painting on his easel. There was no identifiable object in it, nothing but a melange of colors arranged in a most beautiful design. He looked more closely and saw that it was one of his own unfinished landscapes, which for some reason he had left lying on its side. At that moment, he wrote, he realized that he was no longer bound to paint a subject from so-called real life.

72

Kandinsky, Kasimir Malevich, Vladimir Tatlin, El Lissitsky, Alexander Rodchenko and Naum Gabo—the foremost Russian pioneers of Non-Objective Art—began their experiments before the Russian Revolution, and continued to work in Russia for a few years afterward, in the brief period when the fledgling Soviet state was still open and receptive to their new and exciting ideas. But by 1920 the U.S.S.R. had turned repressive, and many of the artists left for Germany and France. The few who returned to Russia, like Malevich (who died in the Soviet Union in 1935 virtually unknown), had their work confiscated and destroyed as "degenerate" by the Communist régime—the same fate that befell Abstract works in Germany some years later under the Nazis. The first wave of Russian Abstract Artists continued to pursue and develop their visions through the 1930s, World War II and beyond, but always in exile.

In 1915 a small congregation of artists in Holland—Piet Mondrian, Theo Van Doesburg, Bart van der Leck, among others—formed a group called *De Stijl* (The Style). They called themselves Supremacists, a term that arose from their ambition to contribute to the formation of a social Utopia based on "supreme" principles of abstract form and order, a

Liubov Popova: Untitled,
Gouache and graphite on heavy paper, 1921–22, 16 × 11"
Courtesy of: Rachel Adler Fine Art, New York

purity of inner vision which, realized on their canvases, might by example free their society from the corrupt pursuit of power and money. Like all serious artists before and after them, the Supremacists believed fervently in the power of art to create a new culture and change the world. It might be said that they painted what the *soul* saw, a spiritual vision which owed no allegiance to any established rule of painting, and therefore pushed painting itself beyond its old reliance on recognizable images.

On the other hand, at the same time the Russian and Dutch pioneers were venturing into pure abstraction, in France a loose affiliation of artists was coming up with Representational Abstraction. The Cubists—Picasso and Braque, Juan Gris and others—were the precursors of this school. Working onward from the increasingly stylized, simplified landscapes and still-life's of Post-Impressionists such as Cézanne, the Cubists, as I have shown in the previous chapter, never completely abandoned real subjects and objects drawn from the natural world. They began with landscapes, still-life's or human figures and *abstracted* (the root of the word means "to pull out") basic shapes and colors, the *essence* of whatever lay before them. The object can always be identified, no matter how much the Representational Abstractionist's emotional vision distorts it. Picasso, who soon abandoned the strict rules of Analytical Cubism, kept to Representational Abstraction for the rest of his life, as did his great competitor Matisse. Neither of them made the plunge into pure, non-objective art

In 1913 the famous Armory Show in New York City brought European Modern Art for the first time to the United States.

It provided Americans with their first view of the work of Paul Cézanne, Henri de Toulouse-Lautrec, Georges Seurat and Vincent van Gogh. The paintings of these Post-Impressionists were radical enough for New Yorkers who had only just begun to accept Impressionism. But the Armory Show also included works by Cubists and other Abstractionists, and these were considered too extreme. Frank Crowinshield, looking back to 1913 in an article for *Vogue* written in 1940, emphasized that the show was completely misunderstood and called scandalous. As had happened in Paris almost exactly forty years previously, when the Impressionists first exhibited their work, the critics who attended the Armory Show were enraged. The largest and boldest of the Cubist canvases was Marcel Duchamps's *Nude Descending a Staircase*, and it made the critics froth at the mouth.

Kenyon Cox, writing for the *New York Times*, called the Armory Show ". . . pathological, hideous . . ." and went on to claim that ". . . these French painters are simply making insanity pay." The *New York Herald*'s critic stated, "Such art should be swept into the rubbish heap, since these men have no claims whatsoever to creating works of art." Sculptures by Brancusi and Archipenko, now regarded as masterpieces, were referred to as "junk." When former president Theodore Roosevelt viewed a Lehmbruck figure titled *Kneeling One* (now in the permanent collection of the Museum of Modern Art), he stated emphatically, for all to hear, "I can control my admiration for *that!*" He also announced that the Cézanne painting at the show was not art, that Malevich's black square, the Duchamps *Nude Descending a Staircase* and Matisse's blue painting were disgraces.

Of course TR is not exactly known for his art appreciation, but his comments certainly reflected the majority of public opinion. Yet despite critical and public outrage—or maybe because of the sensation it caused—the Armory Show had an enormous impact. People came in droves to see the "decadents" and the "wild men," and if they'd come originally to jeer, a significant number wound up cheering. The Metropolitan Museum bought the Cézanne canvas TR hated, and soon after the show closed a few New York galleries began to exhibit Abstract art. The art public's appetite for the bold new experiments had been whetted. It can be safely said that the Armory Show began the long but inexorable process by which New York eventually replaced Paris as the center for avant-garde art. The seeds sown in 1913 would eventually bloom into institutions such as the Museum of Modern Art, founded in 1929, and the Solomon R. Guggenheim Museum, which was originally set up in 1937 (long before it moved uptown to its present Frank Lloyd Wright building) as the Museum of Non-Objective Art. The Whitney Museum mounted its first show of Abstract art in 1935. Although most of the Abstract works exhibited in New York museums and offered for sale in galleries during the twenties and thirties came from European artists, a group which included Burgoyne Diller, Ilya Bolotowski, Fritz Glarner and Balcom Greene, working in New York during the 1930s, produced Geometric Abstract pieces, influenced by the earlier works of the Russians and the Dutch.

But it was only after the Second World War, in the late forties, that Abstract Art was fully taken up by American artists.

2: ABSTRACT EXPRESSIONISM IN AMERICA

The Abstract artists who began to work in the post-war years, mostly in New York City, created America's first important movement in the history of art. Although it drew upon European antecedents, eventually it developed into something entirely unique, and wound up influencing the many European artists who came to the United States during the period, some to escape political tyranny, some out of a burning curiosity to see what the brash American artists were all about.

It was in the forties that Robert Motherwell, Jackson Pollock, William Baziotes and other young artists began experimenting with new ways to express themselves. As with the older generation of European Abstractionists, emotion was paramount. But the Americans went further, rejecting *all* influences—even the rules of geometry and the theories of pure form—from the world outside their heads. There was no prior concept, no planning, only the primal expression of the artist's feeling at the time he confronted his blank canvas and began to work.

When the first paintings of these artists began to cause a stir in New York, critics, though far more receptive to experimentation than their predecessors who had jeered at the Armory Show a generation before, were divided about what to call the new movement.

Harold Rosenberg, writing for the *New Yorker*, called it Abstract Expressionism, or Action Painting. For Rosenberg, the new works were visual autobiographies of their creators: everything in an artist's life which had brought him to the expression, the action, the moment of a given painting was visible on the canvas. The painting told everything about him.

Clement Greenberg, art critic for the influential magazine *Partisan Review* and one of the first champions of the movement, called it Color Field Painting. It was also known as the New York School, because the artists involved were a fairly tight-knit group working and living in and around New York City.

Abstract Expressionism is the term which has lasted, and I'll stick with it. The Abstract Expressionists all knew one an-

other, and met frequently to discuss with passion the move-
ment they were founding at legendary watering spots in
Greenwich Village. The most famous of these was the Cedar
Tavern, where painters like Mark Rothko, Adolph Gottlieb,
Robert Motherwell and Barnett Newman would stay up into
the wee hours analyzing, moralizing and drinking. Another
place was the "Club," a loft where painters and sculptors,
along with the critic Harold Rosenberg and the dealer Leo
Castelli met to talk and drink together. The Chelsea Hotel
Bar, a little further uptown, was another meeting place, where
ideas and passionate convictions about the state of art and
its future flowed as freely as the drinks. Abstract Expressionism was a philosophical and social movement as well as an
artistic one, and the passions at the Cedar Tavern were
certainly as large as those which electrified Les Deux Magots
or La Coupole in the 1920s, the famous Parisian bars where
another generation of iconoclastic free-thinking artists and
writers had gathered to thrash out their theories of art
and life.

Though it was influenced by European Abstraction, Abstract
Expressionism was extreme even by European standards.
Subject matter, as I've said, was banished altogether, and
what was left was wild, a pure celebration of the artist's instinctive and individual interaction with his or her materials.

I've always thought the movement sprang in part from the
growing American interest in Freudian and Jungian psycho-
analysis and in ancient Asian mystical philosophies, both of
which first found widespread interest here in the immediate
post-war years. The young artists came from a generation
which had lived through the physical and emotional poverty

of the Great Depression and endured the turmoil of World War II, only to be plunged into the uncertainties of the Cold War that followed it. In the late forties and fifties, the ever-present threat of nuclear catastrophe created a national paranoia in this country, despite its new prosperity. Conformity to a bland way of life based on patriotism, consumerism and the corporate structure was the rule, and it was high time for artists—always outsiders in any society, and now inspired by Eastern mysticism and Western theories of the psyche—to destroy the social conventions that stood in the way of self-discovery. The Abstract Expressionists were concerned with pursuing a glimmering hint of a more profound level of existence, which, in their view, had little to do with the prevailing platitudes.

Jackson Pollock, the artist most widely identified with the beginning of Abstract Expressionism, was extreme in every sense of the word. He was a violent, self-destructive alcoholic who died in 1956, at the height of his creative powers, in a car crash which happened because he was driving drunk. He had regular sessions with a Jungian analyst who urged him to cut loose from the inhibiting emotional legacy of his restrictive mother and follow his artistic intuition spontaneously, working out on canvas the conflicts which tormented him.

In 1947 Pollock was working with William Baziotes and Jerome Kamrowski in a shared studio, and one day he abandoned the traditional easel and put a large canvas on the floor. The three artists began to fling, drip and dribble colors across the canvas, working strictly from their moods at the time. The collaboration didn't last long, but Pollock had found his abiding means of direct expression. In his famous "drip paintings," he swirled, hurled and splattered his paints—ordinary house painter's enamels—directly from their cans onto the floor canvas. He worked only "in the now," following his feelings of the moment. But this is not to say Pollock's work was random or arbitrary. Remember that he was a trained, highly skilled artist who had produced many realistic paintings and drawings before turning to "Action Painting." The spontaneity which produced the drip paintings was always informed by Pollock's ingrained sense of design and balance. His improvisations on canvas can be compared to the musical improvisations of the great jazz musicians of the period: as with art, jazz in America in the post-war years was breaking away from older traditions, and its emphasis on spontaneity and the expression of the self in the moment of creation certainly influenced Pollock and the other Abstract Expressionists.

The most prominent Abstract Expressionists, in addition to Pollock, are Ad Reinhardt, Phillip Guston, Barnett Newman, Willem de Kooning, Hans Hoffman, Arshile Gorky, Milton Avery and Clyfford Still, all members of a generation born between 1906 and 1915. As you can see by the illustrations, their work was quite different from Pollock's drip paintings: what they had in common with Pollock was energy, spontaneity, the sense of working "in the now."

For example, Clyfford Still might execute a huge canvas consisting of slashes of yellow or white springing out in sharp points from a black field. Ad Reinhardt, whose early work was far more formal and less violent than Pollock's, eventually reduced his canvases to rich black surfaces in which shapes can only be discerned by exquisitely subtle variations on basic black. Phillip Guston began as an Abstractionist, but in later years his work became linear, as his profound involvement with Zen Buddhism directed him toward a mystical minimalism. Eventually, recognizable images, darkly whimsical,

Philip Guston: *Fable II*,
Oil on board, 1957, 24⅝ × 35¼"
Courtesy of: McKee Gallery, New York

reappeared in his most recent canvases. The rest of the American Abstractionists had similarly individualistic styles, and indeed, as with late Guston paintings and most of the work of Willem de Kooning (notably his powerful paintings of women), some of them never entirely abandoned "real" subject matter.

To reemphasize what I have said about the solid formal grounding in realistic techniques which all the Abstract Expressionists possessed, I should mention that Milton Avery, Mark Rothko, Barnett Newman and Clyfford Still were employed, during the Depression, by the Works Project Administration. Established in 1935 to provide work for artists and craftsmen, the WPA commissioned large, realistic murals and canvases for government buildings, notably post offices throughout the country.

Harold Rosenberg wrote that Abstract Expressionism was not a formal school. There was no unifying style, no harmonious ideology. What the artists shared was a celebration of subjective reality, an insistence upon the inner experience of the moment, a philosophy the French writers Albert Camus and Jean-Paul Sartre called Existentialism. Angela Kingsley, in her book *The Turning Point*, provides biographies of the leading Abstract Expressionists, and I found her description of the emotional and intellectual preoccupations of the artists gave me a deeper understanding of their work.

⁓

The event that electrified the art world in 1950 was Jackson Pollock's one-man show at Betty Parsons's gallery in New York. Pollock's success brought his fellow Abstractionists into the mainstream. Critical acceptance created a demand for Abstract Expressionist works, and prices, naturally, went up.

The creative energies of the artists peaked in the early 1950s, but by the time Pollock died, in 1956, the New York School had already begun to fragment. I find it ironic that although Abstract Expressionism had lost much of its initial vitality after 1956, it was only in the later fifties that the individual artists achieved celebrity and got rich.

The irony was not lost on the artists themselves. Clyfford Still, Mark Rothko, Barnett Newman and other important Abstract Expressionists with a spiritual bent actually became fearful of their fame, worrying that the praise and money showered upon them might corrupt the purity of their original intentions.

Rothko, in particular, drew inspiration from profoundly mystical feelings, and initially, I didn't "get it." I remember friends whose opinions I usually shared talking glowingly about the deep mysticism, even religiosity, in Rothko's paintings, but when I stood before the huge masses of color blocked out on his canvases, I couldn't make any sense of them.

I had read about the famous, controversial Rothko Chapel in Houston, dedicated to meditation and contemplation without regard to sectarian bias. It was donated to the city by the John de Menil family, one of the world's greatest collectors of modern art. The octagonal plan for the building was conceived by Rothko himself and designed by the architect Phillip Johnson to accommodate fourteen large paintings Rothko executed in 1955 and 1956.

In 1979 I had occasion to travel to Houston, and I visited the Chapel out of curiosity—possibly I would see what my friends saw in the canvases, although I doubted it. The space itself was impressive, a single, large room, unadorned except by the paintings, furnished with simple benches. I was alone, and I picked a bench at random and sat down. There was no artificial lighting, only the late afternoon sun streaming in through a skylight, mellow and diffused.

I must have sat for a good half hour looking at the deep red and rich black masses of color on the canvas before me, until without warning I felt *embraced* by the painting, drawn into it. With nothing else to distract me, I felt as if all the extraneous baggage and garbage I had accumulated over my lifetime was falling away. It was strange, and quietly wonderful. I sat on the bench for perhaps another fifteen minutes, feeling so still within myself.

When I finally left the Chapel, I saw a sculpture I hadn't even noticed on my way in: a broken obelisk, austere, exquisitely simple, an icon reaching for the sky. It had been executed by the artist Barnett Newman, a Jewish mystic and student of the Kaballah.

Many years later I was talking with the late Dr. Willem Sandberg, a former director of the Stedelijk Museum in Amsterdam. Rothko's name came up, and I told Dr. Sandberg about my experience in the Houston Chapel.

"How interesting," he said. "The same thing happened to me. His paintings never reached me until I visited the Chapel, and to use your very words, it was a spiritual experience. I've felt since that Rothko, Kline, Gottlieb and definitely Newman intended their work to be seen quietly alone, in an empty space like a chapel, or even in one of the smaller galleries in a museum."

Dr. Sandberg went on to say that Barnett Newman felt that a viewer, looking at an Abstract work of art, should go past the aesthetic experience—design, balance, use of color and so on—into the realm of the spirit. Contemplating an Abstract painting should approach an act of belief: focusing on the three intense bands of color which make up a typical Newman canvas, the spectator should enter a meditative state in which the soul speaks out and informs life with meaning.

So much for my own "conversion" to an appreciation of Abstract Expressionism. I certainly don't mean to say that you have to like it, or that you must appreciate the spiritual concepts behind it. But once again, some knowledge of what this group of artists was trying to achieve with their startling break from the world of recognizable objects will help shape your opinion—and certainly take you beyond the limited vision of the person who claims a six-year-old could paint a Pollock.

Your own taste, I keep saying, must be your guide. You may wind up loving the work of Rothko or Still, but find yourself less enthusiastic about de Kooning, or vice versa. It isn't because any of the three is a "better" artist. But every artist has a message to convey, I believe, and it's that message—profound or superficial, depending on how *you* receive it—that must color your judgment. Particularly with the Abstract Expressionists, some messages will speak to you, and some won't.

From the time of the cave paintings, every true artist had felt that she or he has something vital to say, something that will reveal to the rest of us what goes on in the human heart, something that will expose society and point out what is wrong, banal, evil, and what might be changed to make things better. Real artists—composers, writers, performers, as well as painters and sculptors—all begin with a sense of mission, a driving impulse to change the world through their work.

The Abstract Expressionists in America were certainly inspired by their mission to break through the strictures of their repressive society and celebrate the inner vision of the individual. But the lasting power of their work is based not only on their vision, but on the technical skill, born of long practice, which they used to achieve it. I'll give James Johnson Sweeny, the great museum director, the last word: if an Abstract canvas is not "good art," with all that phrase implies, it is merely decorative wallpaper.

3: OP ART

Another spoke in the wheel of Abstract, Geometric or Non-Objective art is *Optical Art*, or *Op Art*, as it is more familiarly called. As the term implies, Op Artists specialize in creating three-dimensional visual illusions, using color and form, independent of subject, to alter perspective. Op Art was a minor, short-lived Non-Objective movement of the late sixties and early seventies, that followed the hard-edged paintings of Gene Davis and Kenneth Noland.

Victor Vasarely, the most prominent of the Op Artists, felt that a conventional painting—a landscape, say, or a still-life of flowers posed in a vase on a table—was static. In such paintings, what is there is *exactly* what you see, and no more; whereas in Op Art the eye travels constantly over the surface of the canvas, never stopping at any fixed point. By manipulating perspective and pattern, the Op Artist fools the eye into seeing movement within a three-dimensional space.

Vasarely explored many means to create, in his squares, triangles and circles, a hallucinatory impression of movement. In the late sixties the Denise René gallery in Paris showed Op Art almost exclusively. The walls were hung with standard 12 × 16 canvases, and I recall walking around the exhibition, my eyes constantly tricked into following the moving surfaces, never stopping in one spot, an experience both exhilarating and a little disorienting.

Other artists of the period who succeeded in bringing off this illusion of movement are Jesus Raphael Soto, who constructed seemingly three-dimensional columns; Bridget Riley, the English-born artist; and Richard Anuszkiewcz. Although the Op Artists are thoroughly contemporary, and we think of the movement as a modern-day creation, it has ancient ancestors. Back in the thirteenth century, for example, floors in churches and cathedrals were often tiled in repetitive geometric patterns, mazelike designs which drew the eye in concentric circles. These tiling patterns, originating in prehistory, had lost their religious significance long before the middle ages, and were conceived as purely decorative. Abstract Art in general, and Op Art in particular, lend themselves to decorative purposes: many of our textile designs, bed linens, and the like, were inspired by original works on canvas, whose patterns wound up being used to enhance everyday, utilitarian objects. So many forms and patterns drawn from Op Art have been incorporated into the designs which surround us in our everyday lives that we are hardly aware of their sources any more.

4: MINIMAL AND CONCEPTUAL ART

When we talk of Minimal Art today we must begin with the painting and sculpture of the late fifties: the Color Field painters, the shaped canvases of Robert Ryman and the hard-edge abstractions of artists such as Noland and Frank Stella. Minimal Art sprang up in reaction to Action Painting— the extreme autobiographical work of Jackson Pollock, Willem de Kooning, Bill Baziotes and the other early Abstract Expressionists, who, as we have seen above, used paint and canvas to express pure emotion and exorcise their personal demons. The Minimalists, by contrast, rejected all emotional content in a painting. The canvas *was* the painting: a canvas of pure blue paint is a canvas of pure blue paint, no message or ideology involved.

Barbara Rose, in her article "A B C Art," published in the magazine *Art in America* in 1965, stated that Minimalism glorified "pure nothingness." The reaction against Action Painting's emotionalism began even while Action Painting was at its height. Robert Rauschenberg's 1952 black-and-white painting, and Ellsworth Kelly's red-and-white acryllic canvas of the same period looked back to the Color-Field work of Mark Rothko, Barnett Newman and Morris Lewis. These artists were the immediate forerunners of Minimalism.

When I first looked at a flat-textured, plain red canvas totally void of nuance, I was reminded of Gertrude Stein's famous line about the town of Peoria: "There is no there, there." But when I used the Stein quotation in reference to a Minimal work, a friend countered by saying, "It's the *looking*, the *discovering*. The *concept* is what it's all about."

Sol LeWitt, not a painter in the traditional sense (and he would not want to be described as one), declared, in a 1969 publication from the Museum of Modern Art entitled *Sentences on Conceptual Art*, "Once the idea of a piece is established in an artist's mind and the final form is decided, the process is carried out blindly. The process is mechanical and should not be tampered with. It should run its course."

Essentially, there were three generations of Minimalists, each with a different driving concept. First came the Constructivists we have looked at: Malevich's simple white canvas that appeared in the 1913 Armory Show, Lissitzky's and Rodchenko's abstract forms either in black and white or in pure colors. These artists deliberately contrasted the purity and severity of their designs to the chaos and corruption of the society in which they lived. Similarly, during the same period,

Mondrian, Van der Leck and the Dutch *De Stijl* group restricted their canvases to stark geometric images to express their inner vision of a purer culture that might save the world.

The second group of proto-Minimalists, working in the late forties and early fifties—Rothko, Newman, Lewis, Clyfford Still and Phillip Guston—were mystics, as we have seen. Their form of Minimalism was based on the idea of paintings as meditative objects. By quietly contemplating one of their canvases, the viewer might be brought to a perception of his or her deepest core of being.

The third generation threw out both the social-reform concerns of the earlier Russians and Dutch, and the mystical concerns of the Rothko-Still group. Minimalists of the final generation, beginning in the fifties and sixties and continuing today, deny there is any message in their work. "What you see is what you get." The notion, to most contemporary Minimalists, is that there is something profoundly exciting simply in the work itself, the "object at hand," so to speak: how a piece of rope, say, is laid upon a canvas in a certain way, as in the art of Richard Tuttle, creates a tension which enlivens the otherwise blank space of the canvas.

In the book *American Artists on Art*, edited by Ellen H. Johnson, Frank Stella declared in an interview with Bruce Glaser, "My painting is based on the fact that only what can be seen there *is* there." Glaser added that Stella's statement is the cornerstone of Minimalist doctrine.

Not too long ago I visited the sculptor Bernar Venet in his studio. His work is nonobjective, but in my view does not completely follow the "Minimalist doctrine." His steel sculpture and the oil-stick drawings on paper, each of which is titled *An Undetermined Line*, are austere, yet I feel the artist behind the work: the human quality is there. Venet, like most artists, collects the work of other artists and I noticed a watercolor painted directly on a wall of his studio I asked him about it. It was a "wall drawing" by Sol LeWitt. Not being *au courant* about Minimal Art, I jokingly asked Bernar if he intended to carve out that part of the wall if he moved.

"No, it will stay where it is," he replied. "LeWitt does his 'wall drawings' first on paper. That paper is the work of art, the drawing one buys. His assistant then executes the design on a wall. When I move, an artisan will reproduce that drawing on a wall in my new place. I can have as many as I want. In fact I have that drawing on a wall in my house in the south of France. It's a mathematically designed work."

On another wall of Venet's studio a series of stainless-steel painted boxes sat side by side in a mathematical progression of volume. As with the LeWitt drawing, there were no emotional tones to the boxes, no relationship to anything but what one was looking at. Venet explained that in Minimalism and Conceptualism an artist pushes to the edge to deny and go beyond the rational and philosophical qualities of European art, and to discover, as he works, where the work will lead him.

Warm up to modern Minimalism and Conceptualism, as I came finally to understand and love the work of Mark Rothko. Although Minimalist Art is designed to have no meaning or philosophical undertones, I suppose I can project my own meaning into it. But for me generally the meaning is a nihilism. Of course this is my personal feeling, and as I have said before, it may not necessarily be yours.

At this time in the nineties, I do not see any precise movement or school—even artists working within the large range of Minimalism differ markedly in their choices of materials and their approaches. By contrast to the eighties, today I see no momentary fad is being hyped merely for public consumption, which is all to the good. I see individual artists looking, working, struggling to find their own ways, whether their talents lead to another form of Abstract Art, to Figurative Art, or, perhaps, to a new vision, as yet unknown, that will provide us with still another way in which to understand our world.

5

SCULPTURE

The human urge to create art goes back to our beginnings, and sculpture began at least as early as painting, long before what we refer to as modern civilization. In the caves of Europe, where some 12,000 years ago early humans left bold and mysterious paintings of animals on walls and ceilings, archaeologists have found equally ancient statuettes of female fertility figures, among other carvings made of stone, and even ivory from the tusks of long-extinct mammoths. Humanity's first sculptures were very stylized, but when the Greeks developed their classic civilization, figurative sculpture took over. By the time of the Romans, actual portraits of men and women were being executed in stone and marble.

With the rise of Christianity, sculptors' aims changed. Instead of depicting human beings realistically, medieval sculptors depicted saints, angels and figures from the Bible in idealized, simplified forms to portray the perfect order of the afterlife, where the souls of the saintly lived forever with God.

Sculpture achieved extraordinary heights during the Italian Renaissance, as artists rediscovered the classical art of Greece and Rome. Commissioned by noble families like the Medici, beginning in the late fourteenth century, sculptors made majestic figures of Christ, the disciples, saints and angels to remind the populace of its allegiance to God. Sculptors worked mostly in marble, although the bronze doors of the Florentine Baptistery, cast in deep relief by Lorenzo Ghiberti, are masterpieces of the early Renaissance. Michelangelo was first and foremost a sculptor in marble: his *Moses, David* and *Pietà* are world-renowned. The list of brilliant sculptors of the Renaissance is far too long to cite in any detail: art was everywhere during the period, in small towns and villages as well as in the great cities. I recall going one day by train from Florence to some of the surrounding towns. I wanted to see the early frescoes and sculpture in the small village churches. In all the churches the frescoes were fragile, in dire need of serious restoration, as a result of absorbing the dampness from the stone walls over the centuries, and the early Renaissance sculptures, too, had suffered. To preserve what was left of the wall-paintings and sculptures, they were kept in semidarkness. To see them I had to deposit a few lire in a box which switched on a very faint light for perhaps half a minute. I kept feeding lire to the box and seeing bits and pieces of the frescoes each time the light came on—certainly a unique way to view artwork. But on that first trip I was hindered in my appreciation of the work because I had little knowledge of the period and its artists. If you are planning to visit Rome and Florence, and are interested in the sculpture of the Italian Renaissance, your best bet is to buy simple guidebooks beforehand. Otherwise you may miss some great works in un-

93

likely places—and in any case, having a smattering of knowledge makes a tour of the Renaissance masterpieces much more exciting.

Our large American cities today are mostly dominated by sleek high-rises erected since World War II, in architectural styles both marvelous and dreadful. Occasionally I find myself on a bus crawling through heavy traffic, and if I happen to look up I see the stone carvings and friezes which adorn the surviving older buildings. Buildings of the nineteenth and the beginning of the twentieth century were decorated with intricate stonework, and the nostalgic part of me wonders why we can't design buildings like that today. But of course nymphs, gargoyles and friezes of flowers would look absurd on contemporary buildings. Today is a different time. Our modern architecture is designed for now. Instead of building sculpture *into* their structures, modern architects often work in concert with contemporary sculptors, who create pieces of the correct large scale for the plazas surrounding new buildings, or for the tall atriums inside them. The monumental steel sculptures of Richard Serra, the playful painted figures of Jean Dubuffet, the mobiles and kinetic sculptures of Alexander Calder and George Rickey were all commissioned by architects for particular buildings and specific sites.

Each generation makes its own art for its own time. Before the First World War, for example, every town, every village in Europe and America had idealized statues of soldiers to honor those slain in past wars, or heroic generals sitting on prancing stone or bronze steeds. Memorial sculpture covered the countryside. Today's monuments are more humble. War is no longer perceived as glorious, and the sober, simple black wall of the Vietnam War Memorial in Washington, which bears the names of the more than 58,000 Americans killed, is a poignant tribute to the dead, created by a woman sculptor, Maya Lin, to remind us that the lives of young men and women are too precious to waste, and their early deaths are not proper subjects for grandiose nationalistic celebration.

There are many kinds of sculpture. A *free-standing* sculpture is a three-dimensional form in space, as opposed to a painting, which is a two-dimensional plane. We can walk around a free-standing sculpture, touch it, feel its volume and weight, just as the artist did as he or she worked. For a sculptor always thinks "in the round," so to speak: he or she is concerned with mass, volume, the feel and heft of the material. If you can bring yourself to ignore the DO NOT TOUCH signs (and the eyes of the guards) in museums, rub your hand over a sleek, polished Brancusi, Moore or Archipenko sculpture, or enjoy the bumps, angles and jagged edges of pieces by Rodin or Giacometti. Solid, free-standing sculpture is sensual. It's *meant* to be touched. Consider the thirteenth-century bronze statue of Saint Peter in the enormous Vatican church that bears his name: over the centuries the bronze has acquired a deep greenish-black patina—except for the saint's right toe, which is the red-gold color of the whole statue as it was when it came out of its casting. The toe has been kept polished through the years by the hands and lips of the faithful.

Sir Herbert Read states in his book *The Art of Sculpture* that painting is an art of seeing, but sculpture is an art of touch.

Auguste Rodin (1840–1917) is considered to be the first modern master of free-standing sculpture. His only link to the neo-classic sculptors who preceded him lies in the fact that his work carries a message, striving to convey some basic truth about aspects of the human condition. Writers have referred to Rodin as a "psychological artist." Like Cézanne,

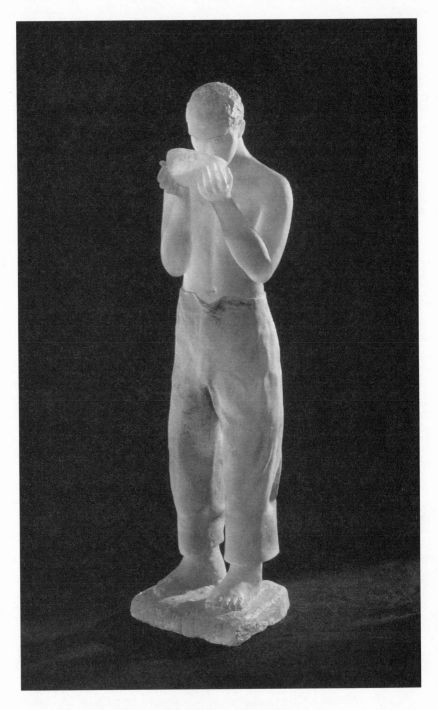

Nicolas Africano, *Drinking from Bowl*,
Cast glass, 1995, 25 × 5 × 6"
Courtesy of: Michael Lord Gallery, Milwaukee

who searched natural landscapes for their inner structures, Rodin sought to bring out the inner structure of the human figure. As Heard Hamilton noted in his *Painting and Sculpture in Europe*, Rodin created the first authentically "ugly" work of modern art. He was not interested in perfect academic studies of ideal figures frozen in time. He instructed his models to walk around the studio, sit down when they chose, rise again and generally behave like normal human beings, while he caught certain eloquent moments of their movement with a few deft lines on his sketchpad. Sometimes his sketches were used to create a complete figure or group of figures, but just as often Rodin sculpted fragments: a torso, a single hand. These fragmentary sculptures are so strongly done that the eye of the viewer fills in the rest of the subject's body. Michelangelo said once in his diaries that his work was to free the figure locked inside the block of marble. Rodin, who worked mostly in bronze, challenges the viewer to complete the figure.

In 1884 Rodin made *The Burghers of Calais*. The larger-than-life grouping shows the chief magistrates of the French city of Calais, who had offered themselves as hostages to an invading English army if its commander would spare the city. Rodin captures the burghers at the moment they learn they are to be executed. A close inspection of the sculpture will reveal that the anguished expressions on the faces of the burghers of Calais, very clear from ten feet away, are rough, abstract angles and ridges of metal. Rodin was edging toward abstraction in this work.

The Burghers of Calais created a sensation among Rodin's contemporary sculptors, though as usual the critics and collectors of his time hated his work. Rodin's sculptural rejection of the smooth, perfect and beautiful images of the human body which had prevailed throughout the nineteenth century was as frightening to the art establishment of the time as the Impressionist painters' slashing attack on formal studio painting had been. After all, the subject Rodin chose had to do with heroes who lost their lives in a war. But they were not shown as heroes. The men are chained together, fearful and resigned at the same time, and they are not even "finished." Rodin intentionally left his final casting rough. I do not know whether the unfortunate men were executed or given a reprieve: the history doesn't really matter. It's the power and audacity of the sculpture that counts.

Rodin's work influenced younger artists enormously. Post-Impressionist painters as well as sculptors took inspiration from him. The Italian artist Umberto Boccioni acknowledged his debt to Rodin when, in 1913, he began to create solid classical forms deliberately distorted to show the effect of motion. Aristide Malliol followed Rodin's example by sculpting torsos without heads—in fact he made a fashion of it. In the truest sense of the phrase, Rodin was the first modern sculptor, and his influence upon sculpture of the twentieth century cannot be overemphasized.

There are a number of casts of the *Burghers* in museums throughout the world, casts done after the artist's death, with permission from the Rodin Museum in Paris. One stands in London next to the House of Lords. In America, New York's Metropolitan Museum and the Los Angeles County Museum have the statue group, and the Canberra Museum in Australia also houses a casting. *The Burghers of Calais* is of course only one of the prolific sculptor's masterpieces, but like *The Thinker* and *The Kiss*, it represents Rodin at the height of his powers.

Sculptors who carve their work out of stone, wood or other materials make only one sculpture at a time: each piece is unique. Artists like Rodin, working in bronze, make multiple editions of their works, and I am often asked how they do it. It's a complicated process, but if sculpture is what you love and may want to collect some day, some knowledge of the technique will help you recognize the quality of a given casting.

The artist begins by shaping a full-size sculpture out of clay. When he is satisfied with the clay image and it has hardened, he takes it to a bronze foundry for the final steps. At the foundry, artisans coat the clay object with liquid rubber to make a mold. When the rubber has dried, the mold is carefully removed from the clay object: the inner surface of the mold is a perfect, hollow negative of the original object.

Next, the foundry workers apply a layer of liquid wax to the interior of the mold. The wax layer is the "positive" image of the original clay object, and it will determine the precise shape of the finished bronze piece. When the wax has hardened, it is removed from the rubber mold and filled with a substance called *investment*, basically a wet mixture of sand and clay, similar to Plaster of Paris. The filled wax object is then placed in a heatproof box and completely buried in more investment, with holes bored through it to the surface of the wax. When the investment, inside and out, has dried and hardened, it is heated so that the wax melts and runs out through the holes. Into the space vacated by the melted wax, the founders pour in bronze (an alloy of copper and tin) which has been heated to a liquid state. After the bronze has cooled and solidified, the outer and inner investment is broken away. What is revealed is an exact duplicate of the original clay object. The sculpture is cleaned and usually brushed with a dilute acid to create a protective patina that keeps the metal from corroding on contact with the air.

Through this "lost-wax" method, the clay original can thus

generate any number of bronze copies. Most bronze sculptors have very close relations with specific foundries, and some of them supervise the entire casting process personally. The artist determines how many copies he or she wants cast—
100 the number of castings of a given piece is known as the piece's *edition* (a word that will be fully explained in the following chapter on graphics). Usually there will be a number etched into each bronze, indicating how many casts of the given piece make up its edition. Today sculptors also etch their names onto each piece, a practice that only originated during the twentieth century: in earlier years artists didn't think their signatures were necessary, assuming their work would be recognized by viewers.

Bronze, of course, is not the only medium used for casting sculpture (glass sculptures by Nicolas Africano or Wain Valentine can also be cast in multiples), and although the technical details of working with steel, chromium, aluminum, etc., vary due to the different melting points of each metal, the basic lost-wax process remains the same as it was when the sculptors of ancient Greece created their great bronzes.

The sculptor deliberately limits the number of casts, because the clay original and rubber mold are fragile and deteriorate when they go through the process too many times. But unscrupulous foundries (and the occasional larcenous dealer) sometimes crank out *sur moulage* copies. The French term means "overcast," and it has nothing to do with the weather. This is how it's done: one of an artist's edition of authorized metal castings is used as the mold to make further copies, edition number, signature and all. How can you tell the difference between such unauthorized copies and the original edition? It isn't easy, but if you compare an overcast with an original edition, you'll see that the overcast's curves and angles, the surface texture itself, appear worn, not as

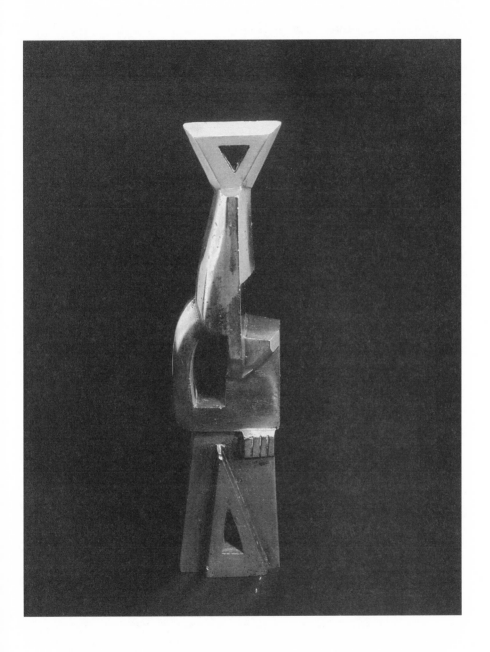

Henri Gaudier-Brezska: *Torpedo Fish*,
Bronze, 1914, Height: 6⅜"
Courtesy of: Gillian Raffles, London

sharp and clear as the original—as you might expect from a copy of a copy. But familiarity with a given artist's work will help to steer you away from galleries selling overcasts, which are fraudulent pieces of work.

I keep repeating: Know your artist, know your dealer, know a given work's provenance (where it's been, who has owned it: I'll go into provenance in detail later on). For now, let me just say that cast sculpture, by its nature, lends itself to fakery, and only experience and a reputable dealer can keep you from being fooled. The asking price for a cast can also clue you in. Not long ago I was offered a cast sculpture by a well-known artist, long dead, whose prices in the art market of the time were astronomical. The offer was at least five times below market value, which persuaded me not to buy it. Bargains don't exist when it comes to limited editions by great sculptors.

Another form of sculpture, today almost entirely restricted to cemetery headstones and monuments since modern architects stopped putting sculpture on buildings, is *bas-relief*. Bas-relief is somewhere between painting and sculpture. It's done on a two-dimensional plane, a wall or any surface of marble, bronze or other material that allows the deeply carved figures to stand out from the flat surface. The great frieze on the Pantheon in Athens, horsemen and celebrants carved so deeply that they seem to break from their marble background, is still a bas-relief. So is a seal ring, or your great-aunt's favorite cameo. But as I said, relief carving isn't much practiced today: if you are interested in bas-relief, you must look to the beautiful examples of it on the walls of ancient cathedrals and the glorious buildings of the classical period.

The transition from the late nineteenth into the twentieth century has been called the end of an age, the breakthrough into modern art, and the same revolution that took place in painting occurred in sculpture. In fact, most sculptors at times turned to painting, and all of them drew. Conversely, many painters also did sculpture: the Impressionist Degas often made small clay figures of his models, to work from later when he painted. The most famous of Degas's statuettes is of a fourteen-year-old ballet dancer, wearing real ballet slippers and a tutu made of tulle. It was not until the 1920s that the fragile clay original and its elements of real costume were found: the statue was cast in bronze to preserve it, and dressed in its original slippers and tutu. It is oh, so charming. Matisse was a superb sculptor, and his busts and figures are influenced by the interest in African art he shared with Picasso, who also created many powerful sculptures in the course of his long and prolific career.

The Italian sculptor Marino Marini, the Russian Ossip Zadkine and the artist whose work I feel so deeply within me, Alberto Giacometti have all painted memorable canvases, in addition to their sculptural work. For the most part, sculptors' drawings are studies for future sculptures, and frequently they are glorious works of art by themselves. The Englishman Henry Moore created innumerable small studies, delicate and beautiful miniatures which despite their small size have the power of the huge statues that eventually came out of them. My particular love is for drawings—I feel they are the bones of the artist—and if you find you share my interest, the drawings of sculptors are well worth examining.

Just as figurative painting began to be variously broken down by the Post-Impressionists and their successors, traditional figurative sculpture changed dramatically at the turn of the century and later. Modern sculptors looked beyond traditional stone and bronze to materials never before used: sheet metal, steel, wire, paper, cloth, plastic—the list is endless. In 1913 the Russian Constructivist Naum Gabo used a brand-new material, lucite, which both reflected light and allowed it to pass through its surfaces. Gabo also began experimenting with sculptures that moved, *kinetic art*, as it is formally known. At the Baltimore Museum of Art he suspended a sculpture in a stairwell: museumgoers climbing or descending the stairs around it lend the piece a spiral movement. Alexander Calder coined the term "mobile" for his exquisitely balanced constructions of metal rods, planes and vanes: even the largest Calders, which can be the size of airplanes (in fact one of the largest hangs in the airport of my hometown, Milwaukee) are so finely engineered that a change in the wind can alter them completely. Once I was waiting for a delayed plane in the Milwaukee Airport, mesmerized by the Calder mobile's huge metal elements very slowly moving above me, pushed by the faint breeze of the air-conditioning system. Suddenly a door opened and a blast of wind accelerated the pieces of the sculpture until they looked like they were flying.

Calder, Gabo, Pevsner, George Rickey, José de Rivera and Jean Tinguely are among the most famous kinetic artists, most of whom, like Rickey, trained as engineers. Calder's mobiles and the work of Rickey are balanced so as to turn and spin by the action of air currents, whereas Tinguely's and Rivera's sculptures are activated by motors—sometimes to alarming effect. In the early sixties Tinguely held a famous one-time-only exhibition of a number of his kinetic pieces, which whirled and buzzed and spun with increasing velocity and noise until eventually they destroyed themselves!

Calder also created small sculptures which borrowed from the art of the puppeteer, the movement of the pieces con-

104

trolled by hand-held wires. For a long while he used to travel with two large suitcases containing all the miniature metal human and animal performers of a circus, putting on performances, manipulating the figures himself while providing a running commentary as ringmaster. A Calder performance of his circus was videotaped and exhibited on screens at the Whitney Museum in New York, and it was wonderful—there were as many adults as children watching the show and laughing with delight.

The kinetic art of George Rickey, by contrast, is austere and elegant, made largely of metal blades in delicate balance, which move subtly as a touch of wind passes through them. *The Sun*, a splendid kinetic work by Richard Lippold, is made of twenty-four-carat-gold-filled wire which rotates in space, sometimes resembling a solid, sometimes a spiderweb with light shining through it, depending on the angle of the sun itself. To sculptors as well as painters, "negative space"— where the solid substance of the object *isn't*—is as important as the object, and Lippold's work bears out a saying of Henry Moore: "A cave is a shape, not the mountain over it."

Innovative European artists as early as 1910 were captivated by the stylized masks and figures of tribal artists, which usually had ritual significance, and began incorporating them into their own work. Picasso's painting *Les Demoiselles d'Avignon* was directly influenced by African sculpture, and the sculptural assemblages he went on to make during his Cubist period can also be traced to his interest in African art. But Picasso was also fascinated by the ancient, "primitive" sculpture of his native Catalonia, and asked his compatriot Julio Gonzalez, who had already begun using traditional Ca-

George Rickey: *Two Lines Horizontal*,
Sculpture, 1973, 16 × 39"
Courtesy of: Geert van der Veen
© 1997 George Rickey/Licensed by VAGA, New York, NY.

Richard Lippold: *Detail of Baldacchino of the St. Mary Cathedral*
in San Francisco,
Photo courtesy of: Haggerty Museum, Milwaukee, Wisconsin
Photographer: Jean Carter

talonian images in his steel sculpture, if he might work with him and learn how to cut and weld steel. Gonzalez's drawings, as strong and powerful as his sculpture, had a strong influence on Picasso's work.

108   Picasso was never averse to working with other artists in order to learn new mediums and techniques. He became interested in ceramics, and visited a master of the medium, Suzanne Ramie, at Madoura, her studio in Vallauris, France. Picasso worked in the Madoura Workshop with Madame Ramie, and between 1947 and 1971 he produced thousands of playful, colorful and mystical ceramic figures, along with pitchers and plates depicting owls, bullfighters and other images from his personal iconography. The majority of the pottery Picasso produced at Madoura is in limited editions. The word "Madoura" is sometimes stamped on the underside of each piece; some are numbered, some not, but there is a catalogue of the *Edited Ceramic Works* published by Alain Ramie that will give you the information you need—date, size, number of copies produced—if you want to buy a Picasso ceramic from this period.

Drawing from a different kind of tribal art, the German Expressionists, particularly Alexej Jawlensky and Nolde, were influenced by carvings from the South Seas, as was Gauguin: to view a Gauguin painting or one of his rare, exquisite wooden carvings is to be with him in Tahiti.

Of course the work of great artists stands on its own, but it adds to our enjoyment if we know something about what inspired the artists to begin with. The break from traditional figurative sculpture in the early years of the twentieth century came directly out of the young artists' rediscovery of "primitive" art: the art of humanity's beginnings, still, at the time, preserved in traditional cultures from Africa to the South Pacific islands and Central and South America. Modern sculp-

Pablo Picasso: *Pichet Grave gris,*
Ceramic, 1954, 28 × 17cm
Courtesy of: Galerie Madoura, Vallauris, France
© 1997 Estate of Pablo Picasso/Artists Rights Society (ARS), New York.

ture owes a lot to ancient sculpture: what goes around, comes around.

⌒

110

The abstract sculpture of the forties and fifties reflected the goals of the abstract painting of the period. Ibram Lassaw and Herbert Ferber were two of the earliest American artists to produce purely abstract sculpture, working in welded iron, wire and bronze. David Smith had worked in a tank factory during World War II and was familiar with all aspects of industrial metal-working. He used fragments of sheet metal and machinery parts in his works, making the point that an artist doesn't need special materials to make "fine art." By incorporating bits and pieces of machinery in his sculpture, Smith shows the influence of the Dadaists, particularly Marcel Duchamps, who simply exhibited "found objects," also called "ready-mades," from the real world—their status as art depended upon the artist labeling them as such. Once Duchamps found an interesting wine rack in a Paris department store. The sales clerk told him it was the last of its kind, because the firm that made it was out of business. Duchamps bought it and exhibited it as a unique work of art. He also exhibited an ordinary, mass-produced porcelain urinal which he hung upside down: the urinal became art because it was shown in a gallery, not in a bathroom.

There are many superb abstract sculptors, from many countries: the Italian Pietro Consagra, the Israeli Yehiel Shemi, the Swiss Max Bill and others too numerous to mention here. Artists such as Loré Riess lived so many years of her life in Japan that her collages reflect her adopted culture. The Abstract Expressionist sculptors shared with the painters a severe, almost

Bernar Venet: *Ligne Indeterminée,*
Steel sculpture, 1990, 269 × 380 × 325 cm
Courtesy of: Galerie Karsten Gneve, Cologne

mystical philosophy, and many of them, like the painters, were involved with Eastern religions.

Most examples of modern sculpture, particularly abstract sculpture, are very large, often commissioned, as I have mentioned, by architects for a specific site. Unless you have a home with a good deal of land, you might want to look into *maquettes*, small casts made by sculptors as studies for their large-scale works. Despite their small size, maquettes by great sculptors are as powerful as their full-size final versions. A maquette of a *Mother and Child* statue by Henry Moore small enough to fit on a shelf in your living room has all the authority and voluptuousness of the enormous Earth Mother figure which came out of it. When I look at a tiny, stick-figure Giacometti maquette, I see Giacometti's passion fully realized: in my eyes, the little figure becomes a ten-foot man walking the earth. Henri Gaudier-Brzeska, an artist who was killed during the First World War at the age of twenty-three, left a generous number of extraordinary small sculptures and drawings. To hold one of his small, smoothly patinated bronze pieces in my hand and run my fingers over them gives me the sort of tranquillity people feel fingering worry-beads. I cannot help but wonder how Gaudier-Brzeska's work might have developed, had he lived longer. When it comes to sculpture, small does not mean less.

As I mentioned, most modern sculpture, particularly since World War II, is too large even for museums, and, in any case, was designed to be seen outdoors. Aside from the pieces commissioned for the plazas around modern buildings, you can find full-sized pieces in sculpture gardens, outdoor settings permanently reserved for the display of large works. The Storm King Art Center, a 200-acre site in Mountainville, New York, boasts large-scale sculpture from all over the world. In Purchase, also in New York, is the Pepsico Collection of Modern Art, another wonderful place to visit. If you

112

go to England, try not to miss the Henry Moore Foundation, at Much Haddam in Hertfordshire, where you will see examples of almost *all* the great Moores placed all over the extensive grounds. It isn't unusual for your local museum to have a small sculpture garden, which displays pieces that cannot be shown at their best indoors. And if you don't insist on the truly monumental, your own lawn or garden can become a special place in which to display sculpture, in a tradition that goes back to the seventeenth century.

⌒

Henry Moore wasn't the only notable sculptor to emerge in Britain after the war, though he is the best known. You might also look into the work of Dame Barbara Hepworth, Reginald Butler, Dame Elizabeth Fink and the startling assemblages of Ben Nicholson.

In America during the sixties and seventies, a time of upheaval and revived social consciousness that verged on the revolutionary, sculptors created a new kind of Social Realism. Constructivist painters, Pop artists, Minimalist/Conceptualist artists had their counterparts among sculptors, who similarly tried to show through their work the mindless banality of the consumer society in America. Andy Warhol didn't just paint Campbell's Soup cans, he cast them in painted bronze as well. Claes Oldenburg's famous "soft sculptures" were made of cloth stuffed with foam: to reflect American fast-food appetites, he "cooked" the world's largest hamburger and the world's largest ice cream cone. Oldenburg once said that he had always been fascinated by the value Americans attach to *size*—the bigger the better. By exaggerating the scale of typically American food, and using soft, literally over-stuffed material, he intended an ironic comment, not just on our eating habits, but on our obsession with size as well. Actually, Oldenburg didn't exaggerate all that much. Just the other day I took a break from writing to have lunch in a coffee shop. Sitting at the counter next to me was a young man with a Reuben sandwich he could barely get his jaws around. Looking at the sandwich, I thought I was in the presence of an Oldenburg soft sculpture.

114

Claes Oldenburg didn't restrict his subject matter to just food, of course. His great innovation was the use of soft material to depict hard objects, and his series of musical instruments (saxophones, trumpets, drum kits) is as delightful as his hamburgers and ice cream cones. In addition, Oldenburg conceived truly gigantic public-space sculptures of ordinary objects blown way out of scale—a toiletbowl float for the Thames River in London, for example, and a set of titanic nostrils to accommodate the two lanes of a highway tunnel in Los Angeles—which were never realized. But the drawings survive, and they are marvelous.

In the sixties, the decade which generated Pop Art, American sculptors like Oldenburg, Roy Lichtenstein and Warhol were generally concerned with making comments about the consumer society in which they lived. George Segal, not usually thought of as a Pop artist, but certainly working from the same ironic attitude which inspired his contemporaries, made plaster casts of living models, clothes and all, and posed the unpainted white casts, often in groups, in typically American day-to-day circumstances. At the New York City Port Authority Bus Terminal, for example, people waiting in line to buy their tickets can see themselves, turned to melancholy white plaster ghosts, standing in a similar line. Like Edward Hopper before him, George Segal is telling a story about isolation and loneliness in an overwhelming, impersonal society.

Sculptors of the sixties and seventies used plaster, steel,

clay—all manner of materials—to express their reactions to the times in which they lived. John Chamberlain uses actual wrecked cars, welded together in gigantic forms, to comment on the American car obsession—and the ghastly annual death rate on American highways.

Nikki de St. Phalle, an American-born Frenchwoman who worked closely with Tinguely, started by making enormous, bloated doll-like figures she called "Nanas," painted in carnival colors, which, to me, carried a message that women were about as well respected as stuffed animals or dolls (in Parisian slang, *nana* is roughly equivalent to "chick" or "babe").

It's hard to evade Christo, the man who wraps everything he can get his hands on. He's packaged the Pont Neuf in Paris, the Reichstag in Berlin and an entire chain of small islands off the coast of Florida. As with Oldenburg's enormous, impossible projects, which survive for the collector only in his drawings, Christo's most grandiose visions simply can't be done—and even if they were, a collector could hardly buy the wrapped Pont Neuf. But Christo is a marvelous draftsman, and if you can find a Christo drawing or architectural rendering, even for a project that never wash done (he once wanted to wrap all of New York's Central Park: the city turned down the proposal but the drawings survive), it's well worth buying.

The American Duane Hanson, born in 1923, was influenced by Segal's plaster-cast figures, but he used polyester, resin and fiberglass on his realistic human figures to produce a fleshlike texture and surface. Hanson's work comments not only upon the vulgar materialism of our time, but also on our hypocrisy. Like Segal, he coated his models with his brew (they must have been patient friends), and the coating captured every detail of the skin of his models, right down to pimples, freckles and birthmarks. Hanson displays his life-size figures with wigs made of real human hair, realistic glass eyeballs, real clothes and, in the case of the women figures, partly chipped nail-polish. These statues are *us*, tired, maybe overweight, dressed in clothes from the mall, and usually in dire straits.

116

Hanson burst on the art scene in 1963. His early work was a brutal response to an American society which cares nothing about its outcasts. *Abortion* shows a dead girl covered with a bloody sheet, a victim of a quack abortionist in the days before *Roe v. Wade*. Hanson also created *Gangland Rape*, which is exactly what the title suggests; *Bowery Derelicts*, a grouping of desperate homeless men; and many other savage works. Hanson's commentary on the social miseries of American society in the affluent sixties was chilling, and certainly not attractive to most established dealers or their clients at the time.

Locked out of the art establishment, Duane Hanson got a job teaching art at a community college in Miami, Florida, and went on making his sculptural pieces. In 1968, Ivan Karp, of the OK Harris Gallery in New York, took an interest in Hanson's work, and the sculptor came back up north. Karp gave him a show, and Duane Hanson passed into art history. I don't know Ivan Karp personally, but he is one of the dealers I respect enormously. Duane Hanson was only one of the many unknown artists Karp supported: to this day he visits fledgling artists' studios and often takes risks by giving talented unknowns an arena in which to show their work

Not long ago I went to an exhibition of Hanson's later work and realized that he had cooled down. His sixties fury against social cruelty had turned into still powerful, but understated satire, targeting mindless consumption. Standing or sitting around the gallery were six or eight life-size figures. One of these figures was an overweight woman shopper in shorts and

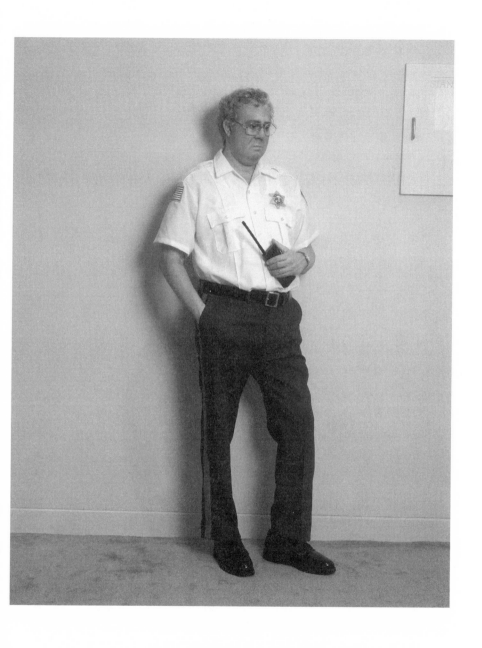

Duane Hanson: *Security Guard*,
Polyester, resin and fiberglass, 1989, Life-size
Courtesy of: Mrs. Duane Hanson, Florida

a T-shirt, the curlers on her hair half-covered by a scarf, pushing a shopping cart overloaded with artificially sweetened dry cereal, sodas, candy and other junk food, everything accurate down to the details of the brand-names and the packaging. As I was leaving the gallery I noticed there was a uniformed security guard posted next to the door, and I wondered why. One can hardly pick up a Hanson sculpture and walk out with it. I decided to ask the guard why he was there, and it was only when I was practically on top of him that I realized the joke was on me. That's right: he was made not of flesh and blood, but of polyester, resin and fiberglass. It was a great touch.

Two other innovations in modern sculpture became important, starting in the late sixties. The first is usually known as *Earthworks*. Sculptors who are very concerned with the preservation of the American environment, particularly its remaining wild lands, find a site in the woods, on an unspoiled river or pond, in the desert or the mountains, and make an object there, out of natural material gathered on the site, which reflects and enhances the site. These Earthworks, made of twigs, rocks, sand, shells and, yes, earth, suggest the art of the Native Americans, and they are not meant to last forever. Some artists have made Earthworks on a small scale and brought them into museums. But inside the museum, these pieces look artificial. Earthworks are designed to be seen on the site, last for maybe a season, and then be absorbed back into the natural setting like a fallen tree or the bones of an animal.

As with Conceptual Art, Earthworks can't be collected, and are not meant to be. But most sculptors who make

Earthworks are good photographers and draftsmen, and the photos and sketches of their work on the site are available. Best, though, if you have the time, is to visit Earthworks on their sites.

Minimal sculpture was the other innovation which arrived during the late sixties and is still produced today. Earlier I mentioned a simple string arranged in a precise manner on a plain white canvas. It is the work of Richard Tuttle, and the notion is that the arrangement of a string in a certain way changes the space of the canvas, and also turns the piece of string into something more important. Similarly, the arrangement of Dan Flavin's ultraviolet and fluorescent lights, which aren't just displayed on a wall, but envelope the entire space of his exhibitions, change the way we see a room.

Richard Serra's site-specific sculptures, massive slabs of heavy steel three stories high, look dangerous, and indeed they are, socially, at least. When a massive Serra, *Tilted Arc,* was installed in Lower Manhattan at Federal Plaza there was a fury of protest from citizens and politicians, which filled daily columns in the New York papers for months. The Serra piece was very large, tons of material balanced in a way that looked precarious, and it was not "pretty." In short, it was very well designed for its location. But people having business with the police or the courts—lawyers, judges, participants in civil suits, members of juries, thousands of clerical workers, whatever side of the Justice system they were on—just simply hated *Tilted Arc.* Federal Plaza became a downright gloomy place in which to take a lunch break, once Serra's sculpture was installed—and the problem was that Federal Plaza was the only outdoor public space convenient to the courts. Now *Tilted Arc* is gone. The controversy surrounding its removal is more a political than an artistic matter. This is simply an example of a piece that was *too* site-specific. I won't vote one way or another on Serra—you have to decide yourself—but the uproar over *Tilted Arc* reassured me that art is still important enough to make people argue about it.

Think of Minimalist sculpture this way: if you throw your coat over a chair, it is no longer just a chair, and your coat is no longer just a coat. You are looking at something that has been changed by placing something else on it. Both have been transformed.

120

A number of years ago I was invited to dinner at an artist's loft. Not very much had been done to repair the place. It still had the old uneven wooden planked floors from the nineteenth century, when it had probably been a warehouse or a factory. The dining table was set up toward the back of the vast space, and as I walked toward it, I noticed a brick on the floor and kicked it aside, thinking that someone might fall over it. A man behind me whispered, "Jeanne, that brick you just kicked out of the way is a Carl André sculpture."

I won't dismiss things I don't understand. Despite the politicians, there are more artists, working in more media, than ever before in human history. But of course I'm back to the old question: What is art? If I mistake a Carl André sculpture for a plain old brick, maybe it's my fault for not seeing it clearly enough, or maybe it's the artist's fault for not making the object precise enough to let me see his own vision.

This brings me to a rather off-putting conversation I had recently, with someone I had thought of as sophisticated, in the best sense of the word. When I told her I was writing this book, and that certainly Pop Artists had a place in it, she became angry. Warhol, she said, and "those kinds of artists who call a soup can art," are frauds. I tried to explain to her what Warhol's soup cans, and Pop Art in general, were about, and I told her she certainly wasn't *required* to like it. But I had to say that to look at anything and declare it a fraud without at least learning enough about it to understand where it came from, was—well, I wanted to say "ignorant," but I just said "unfair."

Modern sculpture, like modern painting, depends absolutely on the eye—and the hand—of the beholder. There is no absolute answer to the question "What is art?" What appeals to the viewer is art. If I love a tiny maquette by Henry Moore or Giacometti, for me, that is art. If I prefer a grand, harsh abstract sculpture in a public place, that is art. If a canvas with a thread hanging from it does something for me, that's art too. I once asked a friend how he would define art. He answered with the old tried-and-true: beauty and truth. But what is beautiful to him may be ugly to me. And truth? What's on the canvas, or in the work of sculpture, is the *artist's* truth. It may be your truth, or maybe not—but it is *not* a universal truth.

Still, to repeat what I said at the beginning of this book, the more art you see, the more you will learn—and the more you learn, the more your concept of beauty and truth will expand and change.

6

CLEARING UP THE GRAPHICS MYSTIQUE

*I*n no medium of the visual arts have there been more opinions, facts, information and misinformation dispersed than in the field of graphics. People worry about the "originality" of graphic works, because, like certain sculptures, they are done in editions, or series. Frequently asked questions include, "What is an original graphic? How can it be original, if there are fifty or more? I've heard a graphic called a print—I thought a print means a copy: does the artist make each one himself? Isn't graphic work less important than a painting on canvas, because it isn't original?"

When someone says, "I only want *original* art on my walls," that invariably means, "I want oil paintings—one-of-a-kind works." It's a common misunderstanding. A one-of-a-kind picture may not be original at all: it could be a copy. *Webster's Tenth Collegiate Dictionary* defines "original" as that *from which a copy, reproduction or translation is made*, and this goes for graphics as well as paintings and sculpture.

The source of an original work of art lies in the imagination of the artist. It's the initial idea or concept—the inspiration—which he may proceed to develop and change, either deliberately or through sudden insight while he is doodling, say, or eating dinner. His first consideration, after the idea is born, is how to realize it: should it be a painting on canvas, a drawing on paper, a collage? Or should it be a print? No matter what the medium, the idea for the work is the artist's own—and that is what makes even a print in an edition of 300 original.

Of course "original art" is *influenced* by the artist's cultural baggage. His vision is shaped by his knowledge of art history, for example. Inspiration doesn't operate in a void. When I look at a late painting by Mondrian, I realize that the modern Dutch painter is drawing on a geometric motif that goes four hundred years back to perspective details in the paintings of the Renaissance master Piero della Francesca. This is not to say that Mondrian *copied* Piero, any more than Picasso copied African masks in his *Les Demoiselles d'Avignon*. But certain elements in the older art inspired the later artists to incorporate them in their own visions.

A better word than original to describe a one-of-a-kind work of art is *unique*—that is, *singular*. Something is either unique, or it's not, and the word can't be qualified—although I myself, in conversation, have made the common error of referring to a "pretty unique idea." No such thing.

A graphic work—a print, say—is original, because it's the realization, in whatever medium, of an artist's original vision. But it is not unique the way a one-of-a-kind painting is, because, of course, it is one of an edition of prints. In art jargon, we refer to a print, then, as a *multiple original*, meaning that it is one of the original series created and printed (or at least supervised) by the artist, and not a copy made, by photoprocessing or other means, from one of the original edition of the print.

124   When an artist conceives of a graphic work, he must decide if he wants to see the finished piece as a lithograph, an etching, a woodcut, a linoleum cut, a serigraph or an aquatint. There are other printmaking techniques, but these are the ones you're most likely to come across. What's important is that graphic art is a medium unto itself, every bit as important as painting on canvas: to most artists a print is an intimate expression of his or her own vision.

My education in art began with graphics, which made up the majority of what we offered at E. J. Korvette. We handled the graphic work of the finest nineteenth and twentieth century European and American artists—Renoir, Mary Cassatt, Berthe Morisot, Childe Hassam, Edward Hopper, Kathe Kollwitz, Chagall—as well as pieces by fine younger artists who were not well known at the time, but have since achieved renown: Leonard Baskin, Luis Cuevas, Phillip Pearlstein and many others. Also, I was fortunate, when I was learning, to have the expertise of Martin Gordon and Peter Dietsch, two of the most knowledgeable twentieth century print dealers. I developed a great respect for the graphic arts, because of the fascinating complexity of the various techniques used. I particularly like etchings and aquatints, but as I have said before about all else in art, this is purely a personal preference.

I'll go into some of the most common graphic techniques, but first I must talk about the great mistake some people make when they bandy about the idea that artists somehow regard their graphic work as less important than their one-of-a-kind paintings and sculptures. It is true that a Rembrandt or Goya etching *sells* for less than the millions commanded by the paintings of these artists, but that's only because their graphic works are more available than their paintings, almost all of which are in museums. The old masters themselves found printmaking at least as challenging and rewarding as painting and, indeed, devoted far more of their time to it. Albrecht Dürer, one of the greatest artists of all time, did almost nothing *but* prints—and if you are lucky enough to find one, and can afford it, buy it! By the time you finish this chapter, I hope you will feel the same excitement I do when I look at a great print. By the way, if you find the following explanations of various printmaking techniques difficult, just skim it for now—if you find you share my love for graphics, one day, when you've learned more on your own, you can return to it and it will make more sense.

125

The oldest type of print is the *woodcut*, which dates back as far as the end of the fourteenth century in Europe, and even earlier in China and Japan. Woodcuts are based on the same principle as sculptural bas-relief. The outline of the desired image is cut into a block of wood with a knife. The artist then carves out the spaces which will *not* appear in the printed image. The raised surfaces which he leaves are inked, and paper is pressed against them, transferring the image. By working with very fine, sharp carving tools, on blocks made of fine-grained hardwood, exquisite detail can be achieved in woodcut prints.

Linocuts involve the same technique, except squares of linoleum, instead of blocks of wood, are used. Linoleum is softer and easier to carve, and therefore more popular with prolific artists—Picasso, for example, made a series of original linocuts that were very innovative and beautifully cut. Because the linoleum block is softer than the woodblock, it wears out faster, resulting, after a while, in a blurring of the prints pulled from it. Hence, Picasso's linocuts, like those of other great artists, are hard to come by, because the editions are small.

The *lithograph* was invented at the end of the eighteenth century. Unlike woodcuts or linocuts, which derive from sculptural techniques, lithographs come from drawing. The artist uses an oil pencil or wax crayon to draw directly on the surface of a square of cut limestone, or on a zinc plate. The stone or plate is then dampened with water, and the oil-based ink is rolled onto it. Of course the water will be repelled by the markings of the crayon or oil pencil, and only the areas that repel water will pick up the ink. For multi-colored lithographs, a separate stone or plate is prepared for each color. The paper sheet is rolled onto the successive stones, picking up the different colors. The stones are then re-inked, and the next sheet goes through the same process.

In order to create an *etching*, the printmaker coats a copper plate with an acid-resistant ground, such as beeswax. With a sharp tool called a *resist*, the artist draws on the ground, cutting through it to the bare copper. The copper plate is then bathed in acid. The acid slips off the ground, but penetrates the exposed lines and surfaces, leaving an image into which the ink will flow. It's the exact reverse of woodcuts, linocuts and lithographs, where the *raised* parts of the surface transfer the ink to the paper. Etchers can control their plates exquisitely: if the waxed plate is bathed in acid only a short time, its lines will be very fine, holding only threads of ink. These lightly etched areas on the plate can then be "stopped out," or protected, with a secondary coating of wax or shellac, to allow a second acid bath to incise the unprotected areas more deeply, for sharper contrast. The copper plate is repeatedly subjected to "stopping out" and more acid baths, until the artist is satisfied with the image.

The ground is then washed off the plate, and the copper plate is polished so that the raised surfaces won't retain ink. The etcher then inks the plate with a roller, and puts it in a press. Porous paper which has been dampened with water is squeezed with great force against the inked copper plate. Only the inked lines cut into in the copper plate are transferred to the paper. You can always tell an etching from any other kind of print by the raised lines of its margins: the great pressure it takes to transfer the image from the inked plate to the paper always leaves a little ridge around the image, caused by the press bearing down on the wet paper. Etchings can be almost photographically precise, because the process is regulated so carefully by the artist. Before the perfection of photography, newspapers relied on etchings for detailed illustrations of important events, but etching as an art form was perfected by Rembrandt, whose copper-plate landscapes have never been surpassed. The Pierpont Morgan Library in New York has one of the finest collections of Rembrandt etchings in the world. I fell in love with Old Master etchings there, and you might, too.

Serigraph is another name for *silkscreen*. In the form it's used today, serigraphy developed around 1930. It's a process similar to stenciling: a sheet of silk is stretched over a frame, and any areas of the sheet not to receive color are blocked out with wax. The framed silkscreen is then placed over a sheet of paper, and the color (water-or oil-based) is rolled over the screen, where it passes through to the paper, except for the waxed areas. Usually a different screen is prepared for each color to appear in the print. Color is more important than line or texture in serigraphs, which tend to appear as flat masses; to my mind the process is less interesting than other printmaking techniques, although Andy Warhol achieved some striking results in the sixties by combining silkscreens and photographs to make his famous multiple images of Mao, Marilyn Monroe and Jackie Kennedy.

Aquatints use a technique similar to that involved in etchings, and are often combined with them. Again, a copper plate is prepared, but in the process, instead of fine lines, whole areas of the plate are exposed to the acid bath. Powdered resin is dusted on specific areas of the plate, according to the artist's design, and the plate is heated from below to make the resin melt and stick. The plate is then put in the acid bath, which bites into the areas not covered by the resin. Very delicate tones can be achieved by stopping out some of the areas with more resin, and subjecting the plate to repeated acid baths. The image in an aquatint appears on a finely pebbled background. In 1969 Joan Miró produced a group of the most impressive aquatints I've ever seen. The edition was small, so today the prints are so desirable they're no longer easy to find. There are many more graphic techniques: I've defined only the most common. If you are interested in investigating further, numerous books on graphic art have been published, and most galleries specializing in prints offer explanatory pamphlets.

The paper the printmaker uses is important, for its texture is one of the values that comes through in the final image. The same figure or design, printed on rice paper or a similar rough-textured handmade paper, will have a totally different pictorial value when it is printed on heavier, smoother, commercially produced paper, not only because of the difference in texture, but because the different papers absorb ink differently. Dimension and margins are other important considerations: a design measuring 5" × 5", printed with a one-inch margin all around, will have a very different impact from the same design printed on, say, a 16" × 20" sheet. The entire sheet of paper, not just the design, is what is balanced in the artist's mind's eye.

When the artist has created the image he wants on his metal plate, stone or woodblock, he then makes his first print and proofs it, examining it the way a proofreader examines a text for errors, to check if the impression is clear enough, if the depth and detail of the lines and the blend of colors are as strong as the image in his mind. If not, he reworks the plate, stone or block and executes another proof. The first proof he pulls is called the *first state*; the expression is used mainly in connection with old master prints. If the artist goes on to alter the design, however slightly, through two or more proof prints, until he is satisfied and prints the final design in a multiple edition, the proof prints are known as *second, third, fourth states*, etc. Rembrandt is known for having executed many trial proofs before he accepted a final version for the print run, and those early states are extremely rare and very desirable to print collectors. The same goes for many other exacting printmakers: often an early state of a print will be marked *état*, the French word for state, to differentiate it from a print from the final edition. When the artist is finally satisfied with the image, he either prints out his edition himself, or, more commonly, turns it over to an artisan who can be trusted to examine each print pulled for quality.

There are some who argue that the artist must pull every print in an edition himself for the prints to be "original," and there are others who say that's nonsense. I belong to the "nonsense camp": if the artist has worked personally on the plate, block, stone or whatever, he has created an original work of art. The artisan, nowadays a professional printmaker whose knowledge of inking, texture, coloring and all the other details of technique usually rivals the artist's own, is ultimately just realizing the artist's original vision. I don't mean to denigrate printmakers: the best of them are trusted absolutely by artists, and often suggest technical changes which enhance the final prints. But *they don't invent the image.*

If, after accepting a final image, the artist decides to do an edition of seventy-five prints, he or she will generally number each print in pencil on the lower-left margin, and sign each in the lower right. When you see "2/75" on a print, it means that this one is the second pulled from an edition of seventy-five, and the artist's signature verifies that he has accepted the whole print run as his or her own work.

To clear up another bit of misinformation, prints later in the edition are *not* less valuable than the earlier ones. 75/75 is as true to the artist's vision as 1/75: the plates or blocks or stones are re-inked by the artist or the artisan after each pull. The value of a print depends absolutely on a clear, strong impression. Never let a dealer tell you than a lower number is worth more commercially than a higher number. Furthermore, I've never been convinced that artists sign their prints in the order that they are printed. Signing prints is a relatively modern custom, and has nothing to do with originality: Rembrandt seldom signed his etchings, though Dürer usually included his "AD" cut into the original woodblock.

Sometimes an artist will include his name, as Dürer did, within the block or plate which prints the final image. It's not quite the same as a signature done by hand on each print, but prints which incorporate their artists' identification generally have more commercial value than those that don't. Of course an edition whose prints are signed individually, after the printing process, are even more valuable: the signature means that the artist has approved of every print in the run.

According to the rule of supply and demand, you must expect to pay a lot more for a print in a small edition than for one in a larger. And artists often reserve pulls of their prints for themselves, for the printmakers, for friends and family. Often these reserved prints can be identified by notations on the print, or on the back of the paper. "AP" is "Artist's Proof." "EA" is the French for the same: *épreuve d'artiste*. If you find "HC" on a graphic work, it means *Hors de Commerce*, French for "not for sale."

Don't be dismayed if you find a print you love with any of these markings on it. If it's in a gallery, it *is* for sale: either the artist has died, or has decided to sell the print after all. If a print is in a commercial gallery, you can certainly buy it. But don't be influenced by the gallery director, who may try to make you spend more money for a print with those "reserved" notations on it than for a regular numbered print in an edition. I prefer the plain numbered prints, actually: at least I know, more or less, how many there are, but I have no idea how many special prints the artist pulled for his printer, friends and relatives.

The usual run of a print edition was once seventy-five (although most Picassos are in an edition of fifty). Artists restricted themselves to seventy-five prints because the plate or the woodblock deteriorated due to wear-and-tear in the printing process, so that prints beyond seventy-five might come out less sharply defined. But some artists kept the run going: they'd number the first seventy-five in Arabic numerals and let their printers and dealers do twenty-five or so more, numbered in Roman numerals. They'd also authorize a further print run done on different paper.

These later runs can make the market for a given artist's work confusing. For example, wherever you go, you'll see Salvador Dalí prints floating around. I don't know if Dalí authorized them or not, but there are editions of his work not only in Arabic and Roman numerals, and on different paper, but there are separate editions for the German market, the French market and so on. This proliferation of editions gives the whole print market a bad name. The practice is misleading and, as far as I am concerned, dishonest. The person who buys a print from an edition of seventy-five, numbered in Arabic numerals, naturally assumes there are only seventy-five "real" prints numbered by the artist in the edition, plus a few artist's proofs, rare prints probably already in museums or collections. The person who buys a print numbered in Roman numerals assumes it is from an edition of only twenty-five. Imagine how the collector who suddenly discovers that there are *hundreds* of his Dalí print must feel.

I don't think artists do this kind of thing today; contemporary artists for the most part keep tight control over their editions. And in any case, today's print collectors are too savvy to buy without asking the right questions. If you see a print you like with an Arabic number, ask the gallery owner if other editions have been done with Roman numbers, or on different paper. And if the artist is well known, you can try to find the print you fancy in a *Catalogue Raisonné*.

A Catalogue Raisonné is a book that contains a description—title, medium, date, size and number of edition—of every print executed by a given artist (Catalogues Raisonnés also exist for paintings and sculptures, of course). For example, Georges Bloch published the Catalogues Raisonnés of Picasso's graphic work. The artist's earliest graphic work, *La Suite des Saltimbanques*, done in 1903, was a series of fifteen etchings, published by Ambroise Vollard in 1913. Two hundred and fifty of them were printed on a paper called Van Gelder, unsigned. There were also between twenty-seven and twenty-nine signed prints of the series, done on Japon, a thinner paper. So in your gallery wanderings, if you run across a *signed* print on the heavy Van Gelder paper, you may be sure Picasso himself didn't sign it. Despite the fact that 250 of each of the fifteen images in the suite were printed—a comparatively large run—many of the Saltimbanques prints are rare and quite costly: two hundred and fifty are actually not very many, when you consider the fame of the artist and the number of museums and art collectors in the world. The *Repas Frugal*, the largest and most beautiful of the Saltimbanques series, has sold for $541,860. *Minotauromachie*, a later Picasso etching (executed in 1935), went for $1.75 million. The finest graphic work of great artists sells very high indeed—though of course a one-of-a-kind work (a drawing, painting or watercolor) of the *quality* of the great *Repas Frugal* will be priced even higher, because it is unique. I've gone into some detail with Picasso's graphics to show you that the Catalogue Raisonné of any renowned artist's graphic work is an important guide: the information about the two kinds of paper Picasso used for the Saltimbanques series, and the presence or absence of his signature, can save you from making a costly mistake. Most galleries offering the graphic work of a famous artist will have a copy of his or her Catalogue Raisonné, and it is entirely legitimate to ask the dealer to show you where the print is in the Catalogue.

There is also the question of *estampes*, or reproductions. These are not part of an original print run, but photographic or mechanical copies, to which the artist has contributed nothing. He has simply sold his permission to a publisher or printmaker, to copy his painting, drawing or print. What makes things complicated is that artists have actually signed and numbered these reproductions, purely for money. A reputable print dealer will mark these signed copies *Après*, French for "after," meaning they are not part of an original edition supervised by the artist. But in the case of signed estampes, all you are buying is the signature, not an original work of art. And a signature alone, on a *copy* of a work of art, is worthless, unless you collect autographs.

I must mention that artists who have signed *estampes* haven't always done it just for the money. A French artist named Jacques Villon produced après of the work of Picasso, among other famous artists. Because the man was starving, Picasso and the others signed his copies so Villon could eat, and I rather like that story—though I certainly wouldn't pay as much for a Villon après as for a real Picasso print.

The world of print collecting is fascinating and, because prints are generally less expensive than paintings on canvas, it's more open to the new collector. But graphic work can be a passion. I know of collectors here and in Europe who can afford to buy an oil or drawing by a world-famous artist, yet collect only prints. Print collectors, especially those who like Old Master prints, tend to become specialists, learning everything there is to know about their favorite artists and the centuries in which they worked. And I've had clients who have devoted a lifetime of study to twentieth-century master etchings. A friend in the Midwest is devoted exclusively to Cubist graphics and has acquired one of the world's greatest collections of them. I also know a couple who only collect the graphic work of the German Expressionists Schlemmer, Nolde, Beckmann and so on. Print collectors are as fussy as stamp collectors: a dyed-in-the-wool stamp collector wants the desired stamp with its original perforations. Similarly, a dedicated print collector wants all of the paper sheet upon which the image was first printed: if the margins are trimmed even by an inch, he won't buy it. He knows that the space the artist left in the margins of his original edition is part of the work of art.

Of course, if you come across a great print by a master which has been trimmed (and make sure to ask about trimming), unless you are thinking about future resale value in the rarefied high auction market, don't let the trimming keep you from buying it. The image will still have great value, as long as you love it and you know what you are buying.

As I said in an earlier chapter, auction galleries can be traps for the unwary. When you go to a print auction, make sure to read the auction catalogue carefully. Graphics are described as "full margin," meaning the paper has never been trimmed since the artist pulled it. If the *measurements* of the margins, *without* the word "full," appear in the description, you can be pretty sure that the margins have been cut down over the years—which considerably reduces the value of a print in the auction market. Make sure to read all the fine print in the catalogue, so you understand the warranties the auction house offers for the authenticity of its works—and be sure to consult a Catalogue Raisonné before you bid on a high-ticket print by a famous artist. Finally, remember that if the numbers of the prints described in the auction catalogue are in Roman numerals, you may be certain that the prints were done in a previous edition which was numbered in Arabic numerals. As I have said repeatedly, at auction, you have to know what you're doing. But with some knowledge, you'll know whether to bid on a print or sit on your hands.

Don't neglect the work of young graphic artists. Because of computer technology, advances in photography and general technological wizardry, graphic art today has gone far beyond the plate, stone and silkscreen techniques of earlier generations. Photographs can be "morphed" by the computer to change them into whatever the artist desires. Multiple-image computer technology can layer a simple image until it looks three-dimensional. Many of the young artists working today make magical use of the new technology—but it's interesting to me that when it comes down to the final print on paper, the best of the new artists demonstrate their mastery of older techniques. I certainly can't say where all this new technology will lead graphic arts in the next century, but I'm very excited by what the latest, computer-savvy generation of artists is up to. The computer, after all, is only another tool in an artist's toolbox—a fancy paintbrush, really.

So for young collectors on a tight budget, let me say I envy you the chance to investigate the new art, take chances on delicious surprises, cultivate new artists—usually for an expenditure of less than a thousand dollars. You're buying new art, and making up your own minds, rather than letting critics predigest your opinions and feed them back to you.

Look around. I keep saying this, but your own eyes must be your guide. Decide for yourself how you respond to the various media in graphic art. Focus on patterns you discover which interest you, and learn about those patterns. Don't just accumulate pictures, and especially, don't just buy signatures.

To give a personal example, after years of living with art, I finally decided that what I like best are the drawings and prints made by sculptors. Famous or unknown, it doesn't matter: there is something that speaks to me about the usually small working drawings and small-edition prints a sculptor makes on the way to his or her final work of art. Sculptors already know about the mass and volume of the work they want to make, so their graphic work tends to be light and linear, suggestive more than explicit. I don't know of any painter or sculptor who doesn't consider his graphic work as an important aspect of his or her art. Fine work is fine work: a good print by a good artist is better than a bad painting made by the artist on an off day. The work of a great artist, in any medium, will always be with us; the lesser work will eventually be recognized as second-rate, and will decrease in value. The crazy art boom in the eighties was an exception: people bought signatures, not quality. I'm glad things are more sensible today.

It's my hope that you will fall in love with graphic art, as I have. It is a grand adventure and less expensive, in general, than paintings or sculptures. One of the things I love about prints is that they are made so that many people can buy them and enjoy them.

137

7

PROVENANCE, AUTHENTICATION AND FAKES

ertificate of Authentication! Provenance! These are the two most important things to look for once you have decided you love a work of art enough to buy it. Without the certificate and the provenance, you'll be prey to foolers, frauds and fakers. To quote Laura Pedersen of the *New York Times*, "Without proof of authenticity your painting may just as well go to a tag sale, next to the eight-track cassette player," if you ever want to sell it.

The *provenance* of a work of art is its history, where the piece has been since the artist created it. Say the artist has been dead for fifty years: who bought the work originally? Whose hands did it pass through after that?

The *certificate of authentication* is a statement, signed by a dealer, which says that a given work of art is a genuine work by the artist in question.

The provenance and the certificate of authentication of a work of art are the responsibilities of the gallery, private dealer or auction house offering the work for sale: these documents, in short, come from wherever you buy the art, along with the bill of sale. If you buy a piece from a gallery, the bill of sale will be on the gallery's stationery, and should give the artist's name, the title of the piece, its dimensions, approximately when it was executed *and* a statement that the piece is an authentic work of art by the artist. The dealer must sign this document, making it a certificate of authentication. The provenance is a separate matter.

In the case of a young artist whose work is usually handled by a particular gallery, there probably will be little history or provenance, so the dealer's authentication is doubly important for your protection. In the first place, if the young artist later becomes well known, his prices will naturally go up. If you decide to sell something you bought when he was just starting out, the buyer will certainly ask for the certificate of authentication. When I buy the work of a young artist, I feel there is no reason a future buyer should know what I paid for it, so in addition to the authentication on the bill of sale, I ask for one on a separate piece of paper which doesn't list the price. The second certificate should also be signed by the dealer, of course.

Secondly, if the artwork becomes part of your estate and your children should want to sell it, the certificate of authentication and the provenance (if any) are as valuable as the work itself. Finally, if by accident a dealer sells you a stolen work of art (and these accidents do happen) and the fact of its theft comes to light, the person who owns it last is responsible for it, and that person is you. It becomes your problem to get your money back from the dealer who sold it to you—and it is then the dealer's problem to collect her money from whoever sold it to her, and so on, until the work is finally restored to its rightful owner. Yes, I found myself in this predicament once. Fortunately the dealer who sold me the stolen work was thoroughly reputable, and he, in turn, had bought the work from another reputable dealer, so my dealer and I were able to recoup our losses. But you can imagine what the third dealer had to go through, tracking down a purchase he might have made years before, to get his money back. Forewarned is forearmed.

Provenances are particularly important when you are interested in buying the work of a famous dead artist—a Renoir, Matisse, Chagall or Raoul Dufy, for example. Master paintings from the nineteenth or early twentieth centuries usually have a history of many owners, from private collectors through dealers to museums. In addition, there are experts all over the world who have specialized in the work of particular artists: they can recognize brush strokes, choice of colors, all the tiny intricacies that identify the hand of the artist. A certificate of authentication from an expert on a given artist is the final assurance that the work is genuine. For example, if I buy a Renoir, I want a certificate from François Daulte, because he is the authority on Renoir.

Last year I bought a Marie Laurençin pastel from a most reputable gallery in Chicago. I had the gallery's guarantee on the bill of sale, but I totally forgot to ask if they had a certificate of authentication from the Laurençin expert in Paris. I hung the picture on my wall, and a dealer friend looked at it and said, "Jeanne, I don't know, I'm not certain about this picture. Do you have the certificate?" I thought for a moment, and said, "No! I can't believe I never asked for it." I called the Chicago gallery immediately. They informed me only that the pastel had belonged to one of the trustees of a Chicago museum, as if that were enough. It wasn't: after my friend questioned it, I couldn't offer the pastel for sale. I wrote to the expert in Paris, enclosing two 5" × 7" photos of the piece. The expert stamped and signed the photos, finally a firm acknowledgment that the pastel was an authentic Laurençin.

And now to fakes. In the memory of all living art dealers, the names of three art forgers stand out: Emyr de Hory, David Stein and Van Meegeren. In 1969 Clifford Irving wrote a book called *Fake*, and in it he referred to de Hory as the greatest art forger of all time. Irving knew de Hory personally: they both lived on the island of Ibiza. De Hory, not a discreet man, told Irving his life story. In the beginning de Hory concentrated on faking Picasso drawings, which was chancy, because Picasso was still alive. After Matisse died he switched to forging Matisses, which was safer. But he is perhaps most famous—or notorious—for his fake Modigliani paintings and drawings. I have seen some of the drawings and they are so perfectly executed, with all the qualities one finds in real works by the artist, that to this day, unless I could bring Modigliani back to life and ask him directly if a given drawing up for sale were really his, I doubt I'd buy it.

The Fogg Museum in Boston, among many other museums, bought a de Hory fake; collectors, too, were fooled by the master forger. One, Alger Meadows, a Texan, bought *forty-four* de Hory forgeries and was delighted with himself because he was able to talk the asking prices way down.

De Hory sold almost everything he did, faking certificates of authentication and using paper from the right periods, from old books and portfolios, carefully splitting them apart to show the identifying watermarks on the sheets.

A few notable dealers bought and sold his work, innocently,

I like to think—yet when de Hory was finally caught, almost all of them refused to testify against him in court. An exception was Joseph Faulkner, a Chicago dealer. When the scandal broke, he not only appeared in court to admit he had been fooled, but also returned all the money his clients had paid him for the fakes. Joe and I spent many a fine evening talking over the de Hory story. He told me the reason his fellow victims had refused to testify was that they didn't want the world to know they had been taken in by the forger. Acknowledging their mistakes would call their expertise into question, and the art market would suffer. I've mentioned above how important it is to get a certificate of authentication from the proper expert when you buy a work by a deceased master— but in the case of a forger of de Hory's skill and thoroughness, even the certificate may be questionable, since he faked certificates as well. It's lucky for the art world that a brilliant forger like de Hory only comes along once every twenty years or so. . . .

Emyr de Hory sold his forgeries for over twenty years before he was caught (for details of his career and the way he was tracked down, I recommend Irving's *Fake* highly—it reads like the best of mystery novels). David Stein, much younger, trying to foist his forgeries off on a more savvy art world, didn't last nearly as long before he wound up in a French jail. De Hory, always an egomaniac, referred to Stein as an *arriviste,* but during Stein's relatively brief career he fooled a lot of people.

You may ask, as I have, that if these men could draw and paint well enough to fool experts with their fakes of other artists' work, why didn't they create their own art? De Hory certainly tried, and he even had gallery shows of his work. But his reviews were not good, and nothing sold. I can only think that what makes a person an artist is his or her creative imagination, plus the technical skill to realize that vision on canvas, on paper or in clay. De Hory and most successful forgers certainly have the technical skills—but they lack the crucial ingredient.

As de Hory's story was Clifford Irving's, David Stein's is mine. In the late sixties, when I was working for Korvette's, a dealer whom I knew and liked—I'll call him Alan—came to the Douglaston gallery to sell me six Marc Chagall gouaches, colorful works on paper in vivid reds and blues, featuring people and animals floating in air, the whole Chagall iconography. They were lovely—and they came with certificates signed by André Pacitti, the ranking Chagall expert. I knew the minute I saw them that I'd buy all of them if the price was right. When Alan quoted me the prices I must have appeared puzzled, a look he took for "too expensive." He said, "You must be joking, Jeanne, you can't say they're overpriced! It's a fantastic deal!"

"It's too fantastic," I told him. "There's no Chagall at those prices. What's the story? They must be stolen."

Alan was understandably upset. "Stolen! For once I bring you the bargain of the century and you think the work has to be stolen? I bought them from a friend of Chagall. Chagall often gives him pieces to sell, he knows the guy needs money. Chagall even has to go behind his wife's back. And as for stolen, the pieces have Pacitti certificates!"

But it still didn't feel right to me. The prices were far too low, and besides, Chagall was not known for his generosity. Still, I told Alan that if he'd check out the gouaches and the certificates with Pacitti, I'd buy them. Three weeks later Alan called and asked me to meet him for lunch. My heart sank: the gouaches must have turned out to be stolen property, because otherwise Alan would have simply asked me to send a check.

We met at a coffee shop, and Alan, who normally just grabs a quick sandwich for lunch, began to go over the menu, telling me what was good. "Try the special bean soup, it's the best," he said. He was making a grand event over what to eat in a three-booth greasy spoon: I knew something was wrong.

Finally I said, "It's OK, so they're stolen. But you haven't actually paid for them yet, have you?"

He looked miserable. "Yes, I have. I paid for all six. But no, they're not stolen. They're fake. All of them. And so are the four Braques I bought from the same guy."

"But the Pacitti certificates," I stammered.

"Fake too. I flew to Paris to show the gouaches and certificates to Pacitti in person. He'd never seen the pictures or the certificates before in his life."

Chagall's "friend" turned out to be David Stein. Alan told the Assistant District Attorney of New York City his story. The ADA, with Alan and two policemen, went to Stein's Park Avenue apartment, but Stein spotted the cops through his peephole and fled through the back door and down a fire escape. He caught a plane for France.

Eventually he was caught, and he did spend a few years in a Paris jail. But after he served his term he went public, painting "Chagalls" and signing his own name to them openly. In fact some years ago David Stein was on television, showing the viewers how he "created" Chagall paintings. Some viewers probably thought it was a great joke. I didn't. My sense of humor fails me when it comes to art forgery, especially when the faker becomes a celebrity after he is caught.

The story falls under the heading "Never Trust a Bargain," which I have talked about earlier in this book. If someone comes to you and says, "I have the greatest deal in the world for you!", ask yourself, "Why me?" More than likely you are dealing with a con man—what reputable art dealers refer to as an odd-runner, someone who can spot an eager, greedy, and not very knowledgeable bargain hunter (like Alger Meadows and his forty-four fakes), who likes nothing better than to think he has outsmarted the experts and bought "great" art for nothing.

Yes, there *are* art bargains. There are times when a collector needs to raise money fast, for whatever reason, and is willing to sell a work of art quickly and privately and to take a small loss on it. And there are people who have owned an important work for many decades, who find their children aren't interested in art. Rather than leave the work to the children, such collectors, working up a will, might sell it for less than market value to give their children cash instead.

But these situations aren't common. Fine art, especially by dead masters, is very hard to come by. And there is always a collector willing to pay top dollar for a quality piece. Unfortunately, within the past twenty years more ersatz, fly-by-night art dealers have popped up than there are paintings by Corot (the nineteenth-century French painter was often faked, and an art-world joke has it that he painted two thousand paintings during his lifetime, of which eight thousand are in the United States).

For example, last year I received a call from a man who said he was a dealer in Florida. He had two paintings by the late Cuban artist Wilfredo Lam, brought to him by a friend who had recently emigrated from Cuba. As much as the friend hated to sell the paintings, I was told, he needed the money to get started in America. Wilfredo Lam was a Surrealist painter, a wonderful artist, and I knew his work well. Over the years I'd sold eleven or twelve of his drawings and paintings.

I told the Florida dealer that I was interested, but I asked him to send me photographs of the two pictures before I would commit myself. When the photos arrived I could tell without further checking that the paintings were fakes.

The point is that you have to spend time with an artist's work, you have to learn to recognize his or her "hand," before you develop an instinct, an inner feeling, for what is genuine and what is not. In the case of the fraudulent Florida dealer, the "Lams" were so crude even their photographs screamed FAKE. But in the case of a more accomplished forger such as de Hory, who even faked certificates of authentication, you can get into real trouble unless you know how to contact the recognized experts on a given artist's work. When it comes to the rare canvas by a dead master which shows up for sale, your certificate must come from the person generally recognized as the final authority on that artist's work. Curiously enough, certificates of authentication are generally harder to fake than actual works of art.

I realize that once again I have been counseling nothing but caution, and I certainly don't want to scare you off buying the work of a deceased master artist altogether. Just be forewarned. Develop a good, close relationship with a dealer you can trust.

So far my counsel of caution has been applied to the work of established, dead artists whose prices are high. The Great Dead are always targets for art forgers, and as I've said above, some of the forgers are very good indeed. You won't have the problem of fakery if you decide to buy the work of young artists. Because emerging artists don't command huge sums in the art market, it doesn't pay to fake their work.

A reputable public gallery or private dealer will never buy a work of art without checking the work's provenance and getting the work's certificate of authentication from an acknowledged expert on the artist. And a knowledgeable collector will never buy a work from a gallery or private dealer without the necessary credentials. If you buy at auction, you should demand the same warranties you get from dealers.

The certificate of authentication is literally irreplaceable. If you lose it, you can't get another and an expert will not au-
thenticate your artwork. It makes sense: if certificates could be replaced, there might be dozens of them floating around the art market for one picture and all its fakes, which would start an expensive game about which picture is the real one.

What I have said above has to do with buying important works of art: pieces by recognized masters, or by young artists you think may become renowned. I'm not talking about attending little country auctions and galleries. I always have a good time at country galleries and auctions, nourishing the fantasy that an unknown Leonardo da Vinci drawing, kept in someone's attic for generations, might show up for five dollars.

Alas, it is indeed a fantasy. Country dealers and auctioneers are every bit as sophisticated as their equivalents in big cities. They know the value of what they sell. Antique furniture, arts-and-crafts, folk art and so on aren't in the realm of this book. But occasionally a piece by a recognized fine-arts master does show up in a country auction or gallery, perhaps because a collector has died and his heirs are selling off his estate.

My niece once went to a village auction where a drawing by Gongorra was on the auction block. She knew nothing about Gongorra, but she told me later that because I had told her he was a fine artist, she kept her hand up at the auction until she finally had the drawing for seventy-five dollars. For some, seventy-five dollars is no big deal, but for my niece it was a major expense. She was delighted until she looked closely at the drawing. The paper was permanently stained.

There was a crudely patched tear in the middle of the drawing. It *was* a Gongorra, but it was in such bad shape it could never be restored.

She was certain she had been cheated, until I showed her the fine print in the auction catalogue. Under the Gongorra it said "as is," stains, patches and all.

148

It's fun to take a chance in a country auction, and people have been known, although not often, to buy a valuable print or painting at far less than market value. The rare cases of an important work of art going for little money in a country auction or gallery generally make headlines on the front pages of newspapers when the story comes out—which should tell you how rarely it happens.

The chance you take on art depends on how deep your pockets are. I can only speak for myself: unless I fall in love with a drawing or a watercolor and absolutely have to have it, I won't spend a lot of money for it. I am a professional art dealer, after all. I'll shrug and let it go.

I have one more story about a grand faker. In 1938–39, in Holland, a religious painting by the Dutch master Vermeer came on the market. There was no record of the painting, and besides, Vermeer specialized in domestic scenes and had never been known to have painted religious subjects. According to Dutch experts, the religious subject was an aspect of Vermeer's work that had not previously been known. They concluded that the painting was genuine, and that it had either been lost or perhaps hidden by the artist himself. The painting became the event of the century among the Dutch art experts.

The Vermeer was bought by the prestigious Boymans Museum in Rotterdam. After the war, during the Allied occupation, more Vermeers turned up. A man named Van Meegeren was arrested on the charge of selling Dutch national treasures to the Nazis. Hitler's Luftwaffe Chief Hermann Goering was notorious for his ill-gotten art collection, and during the war Goering certainly did acquire a questionable Vermeer. After the war, Van Meegeren tried to convince the Allied authorities that although he had sold "Vermeers" to Goering, he'd never sold a genuine painting by the great master. The paintings he sold to the Nazi warlord, he said, were all original Van Meegerens, only *signed* Vermeer.

No one believed him, until, while still in jail, Van Meegeren asked for canvas and paint. He aged the canvas using various clever techniques and proceeded to paint a religious subject in the exact style and technique of Vermeer. He then subjected the painting to heat in order to produce the cracks in the pigment which naturally occur in old master paintings after time.

Van Meegeren proved his point: he was the greatest faker of Vermeer (and other old Dutch masters, de Hoogh and Frans Hals) who ever lived. He was eventually released from prison, but he remained bitter for the rest of his life because his interviewers were never interested in his *own* work. Today, any competent art restorer could recognize Van Meegeren's crude aging processes, but when he painted them for the Nazis, his Vermeers were completely convincing. Van Meegeren died before his case came up. Indeed, I've heard recently that the Rotterdam Museum still has the Van Meegeren. It certainly is a collector's item!

In short, you must find out everything available about a work of art before you buy it. Demand the provenance and certificate of authentication. Without these crucial guarantees, your Vermeer might turn out to be a Van Meegeren, your Modigliani a de Hory, or your Chagall a clever, but worthless, David Stein.

8

CARE AND FRAMING OF ART

The *care* of the *work* comes before the esthetics of the frame. Before you and the framer discuss whether you want a narrow natural-wood frame or a simple gold leaf with a bevel for, say, your Louise Nevelson pencil drawing, you must get to know the framer's reputation. Unfortunately the nice man in "Ye Olde Frame Shoppe" just up the street who turns up the edges of your valuable drawing, or worse, trims it to fit into that antique frame you inherited, still exists, not only in small towns, but in big cities as well. Anyone can set up shop, present samples of frames and perhaps suggest a dark green mat to bring out the green in your picture. What you need is a framer who knows about the proper care of works on paper, as well as the style and type of frame most appropriate to a given piece.

I am not talking about a poster that reminds you of that

quaint town you loved in Mexico, or a birthday card or other message of sentimental value which you might want to hang in your kitchen, side hall or bathroom. I mean fine art you have acquired at some expense—a Nevelson drawing, Picasso print or Fernand Léger gouache—something that you intend to have in your collection for many years and that needs to stay in marketable condition if you ever choose to part with it.

It was only after I became a dealer and found myself responsible for the care and framing of the work I bought that I learned that all work on paper *must* be backed by acid-free paper or rag board and held in place with linen hinges, and that Scotch tape or glued-down corners will cause permanent damage to the art. Among my first purchases as a private dealer were a postcard-sized Magritte watercolor and a Miró drawing, both unframed. These were the most expensive works I had ever owned, and of course I wanted the most appropriate frames for them. But I knew nothing about framing. When I worked at Korvette's, the gallery employed its own framer—and, as I only realized when I began to learn about the proper care of art, he was not good. He regularly trimmed full sheets to fit frames, glued corners down and had never heard of acid-free paper. I heard later from clients that some of the Korvette gallery's works on paper had to be sent to paper conservators to repair the damage the framer did.

It was my good luck that a day or two after I bought the Magritte and the Miró, I happened to go to an exhibition of small gouaches by Max Ernst. I saw that the pictures, about the same size as my Magritte, were in simple white-gold frames, which complimented them without overpowering them. I knew the owner of the gallery where the Ernst works were displayed, and he gave me the name of his framer. I have used that framer ever since, for almost twenty years.

A framer is more than a person who simply measures a work of art and fits it to a frame. If he is good, he is an artisan with a strong esthetic sense who knows that his first duty to a work of art is to protect and preserve it. He will use only linen hinges to hold down the edges of a work on paper, knowing that the acid in Scotch or commercial packing tape will eventually seep through the picture, leaving stains that only a paper conservator can remove, at considerable expense. A good framer uses only acid-free paper or ragboard for his mounts and mats. He knows that the acid residue in most commercially produced paper will, in time, produce *foxing* on the original artwork—those dim brown spots you can see coming through some prints or drawings. Old Master works on paper are generally subject to foxing, not because of their age (the paper the Old Masters used was acid-free), but because collectors and dealers regularly remounted them, beginning in the early twentieth century, on cheap, acid-based paper.

Foxing also develops when a work is not completely sealed within its frame. Humidity fluctuations and marked changes in temperature are the enemies of fragile works on paper, as is exposure to direct sunlight. But the simple flow of air across an unprotected drawing, particularly in our polluted cities, can cause it to deteriorate very quickly.

Foxing, folded corners and stain marks can diminish the value of a work of art. When you consider purchasing a work on paper, you should ask the dealer to take it out of its frame. Often substantial damage is hidden by the work's mat. Don't panic if there is a stain or a small tear in the border of the drawing or print. Fine paper conservators can eliminate stains and even make small tears invisible. But a good framer will make sure such problems won't happen to your artwork. For covering the drawing, he'll use a form of plexiglass which screens out harmful ultraviolet light and he'll avoid plain glass or the older form of plexiglass, which can let UV light in to damage works on paper or fade the colors of prints. He'll also know *not* to use plexiglass to cover pastels and charcoal drawings because plexi generates static electricity, which can lift the particles which make up the drawings right off the paper. And he'll know how to avoid squeezing the picture like a sandwich between the glazing and the backing. Ideally, the work rests on an acid-free paper and built-in spacers create an air space between the surface of the work and its glass or plexi cover.

Though all fine art on paper must be mounted behind glass or plexiglass, the oil in paintings on canvas creates its own preservative. Occasionally you'll see an Old Master painting protected behind glass, because of its age and fragility. Much depends on how the canvas was prepared before the artist painted the picture: some Old Masters experimented with different treatments, and their experiments didn't always stand the test of time. And of course covering an old work with glass protects it from the occasional crazy who feels he has to touch the cracks an old painting naturally develops over the centuries. Many paintings from the early periods have been overrestored or coated with too much shellac by incompetent restorers, to the point that there is very little left of the original works. A certain amount of restoration is to be expected on an old painting, but if it is overworked, the piece can lose much of its value. If you are interested in buying a costly old painting, in addition to getting its provenance, you should take it to a restorer. He will use a "black light," which allows him to see right into the pigment, to find out exactly how much restoration has been done.

Restoration can be a problem even with modern paintings. I have a friend who owned an Ad Reinhardt, a pure black canvas. As with other monochromatic abstractions, such as the work of Rothko, Newman or Kelly, the Reinhardt's appeal depended largely on its surface texture. Every brushstroke showed, and every mark on the surface was important. My friend was persuaded to lend his Rinehart to a museum for an exhibition. Due to mishandling, the painting was scratched clear across the canvas. Since the painting was a flat black image, erasing the scratch would have meant repainting the entire canvas. My friend sold the Rinehart, scratch and all, for a lot less than he had bought it. Needless to say, he has never since lent so much as a cheap poster to anyone.

Of course the esthetic presentation of your painting is important. If your framer knows something of art history and the frames that were typically used in certain periods, he'll be able to pick a frame style that will show your art to its best advantage. It isn't always necessary to use a modern, barebones frame for a modern painting or an ornate one for an Old Master. Your framer should be able to make sensible choices, based on the character of the art. A heavily carved Spanish-style frame on a delicate Renoir watercolor will obviously overpower the watercolor, whereas the same frame on a strong Picasso oil would be absolutely fitting. And a small, finely detailed Rembrandt etching might look better to you in a very simple frame than in the ornate style popular in Rembrandt's own day.

Your framer should be able to offer accurate reproductions of the moldings, carved and uncarved, of many different periods. I've known some framers who will track down original period frames, usually costing thousands of dollars—and worth the price to a collector with a very valuable painting from the same period as the frame. Mass-produced moldings

154

with anodized aluminum, imitation-gold leaf, rather than real twenty-four-carat-gold or white-gold leafing, will look as cheap as they are on valuable paintings. If you have acquired a fine work of art, stay with a quality frame. A simple gold or silver swan frame, or even an unadorned molding in natural wood, looks best on a delicate drawing or pastel from any period and also suits most contemporary paintings.

The frame is the background which presents the art, not a decoration to be noticed for itself. And the mount upon which the artwork rests is an integral part of the frame. Natural silk-covered mats in white, off-white, ivory or very light beige are always complimentary to a work on paper.

As you can see from the illustration on page 156, the margins of the mat should not be the same width as the frame molding itself. If the margins and the width of the frame are too similar, the result will look clumsy. Wider mats usually look better with narrower frames, and vice versa. As for positioning the artwork on the mat, leaving more space at the bottom than at the top generally works better. It's a matter of proper proportion, and your own eye will guide you.

Often, a *liner* is used when framing a canvas. The liner is a fabric-covered, narrow wooden frame *within* the main frame, made to hold the painting when a little space is desired between the edges of the work itself and the inner edges of the frame.

None of these suggestions are written in stone. Of course a painting can be framed without a liner; and some works on paper look stronger positioned squarely in the center of their mats. You must follow your own taste and the advice of a trusted framer—but *not* the notions of an interior decorator. Recently I was invited to the apartment of a couple whose bible must have been the current book on what was *au courant* in home decoration. The hostess had covered her sofa and

Examples of oriental mat proportions:

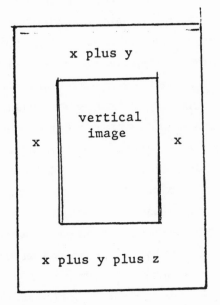

vertical format

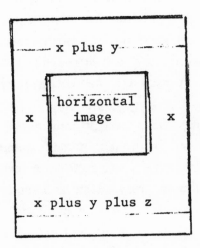

horizontal format

Mat illustration Courtesy of: Mr. Walter Jamieson, New York

chairs in a leaf-patterned fabric made up of various shades of green. The carpet picked up one of the greens in the fabric; the lampshades were in another shade of green; and there were ivy and jade plants all over the room. The green motif extended throughout the large apartment. My hostess escorted me to the dining room, where she proudly showed me her treasures, four drawings all on one wall. There was a black-and-white Bonnard of a woman stepping out of her bath; a delicate and charming Marie Laurençin figure holding a bouquet of pink flowers; a Raphael Soyer pastel of a young girl; and another I can't recall. All the drawings were superb. But each one was surrounded by a green mat, and to further the nightmare, the frames were covered in the same leafy-green-patterned fabric as the furniture! **A work of art is not a decoration.**

As I mentioned earlier in this chapter, not every drawing, print or poster you find in your travels will be a serious work of art, and you certainly don't have to treat a snapshot or an inexpensive poster with the same care in framing and preservation that I have outlined above. I have some delightful prints which I picked up at a street fair in London, and I definitely use them for decoration. I surrounded them with colored mats and framed them in white painted wood, and I think they look great next to the wallpaper in the bathroom. If you have some pieces which are chiefly of sentimental value, not costly, why not use them as decorations? But if you have used your growing knowledge of art to spend a significant amount of money for a fine work, you owe it to the work—and to your own good taste—to mount, mat and frame it in a way that both protects the piece and shows it to its best advantage.

The same advice goes for selecting a framer as for choosing a dealer: don't be afraid of asking questions. "Do you use

Raphael Soyer: *How Long Since You Wrote to Your Mother?*
Oil on canvas, 1934, 22 × 32"
Courtesy of: Forum Gallery, New York, and the Estate of Raphael Soyer

linen hinges? Acid-free mats? Should my artwork be protected by clear glass or plexi?" Ask all the questions I have brought up in this chapter, and any more you can think of. It's the quickest way to find out if you have a trustworthy framer. Once you have a framer you can count on and a dealer you trust, you can follow your own taste in art collecting with confidence, secure in your own knowledge.

9

APPRAISAL, INVESTMENT, COLLECTING

*L*et me end with some thoughts that address the questions you may have come up with in the course of reading this book, thoughts which I hope will add to your confidence and pleasure when you come to the point in our shared journey where you want to start collecting art. Art is not separate from everyday life. It has always been an integral part of human civilization. Whereas civilizations have disappeared, works of art remain if only in fragments and they have always changed as our various cultures have changed. Today as always, we are surrounded by art in many forms, some good, some bad. The buildings we live in, the furniture we choose for our homes, the designs in our daily lives, from flatware to floral arrangements, are all part of the story of art. Even what we eat is influenced by art: in a fine restaurant, the chef knows that the attractive presentation of his culinary creations contributes largely to his diners' pleasure. A bouquet of flowers carefully arranged, food presented with grace and certainly the clothing we wear are all, in their ways, artful. Helping you to become aware of the way art pervades every part of our lives and surroundings is the main reason I wrote this book. The gratification, the pure enjoyment one experiences in living knowledgeably with art contributes a great deal to life's pleasures.

Some days when I am in my library reading, I'll glance up from the page to the small Botero sculpture on my desk. She's an overblown, fat little lady with a tiny head, and she always makes me smile. I may not even notice her the next day: perhaps I'll pass through my living room and fix on the spare lines of Giacometti's lithograph of the *Walking Man*, a piece that invariably brings me closer to myself. I don't know why it is that one day I'm drawn to Botero, another to the Giacometti, still another to, say, a beautiful watercolor of orchids by the Scottish artist Elizabeth Blackadder. The reason is probably no more complicated than the impulses we all share, to talk to a certain person on a specific day, or to pick up a well-loved book and find a passage you cherish. Works of art should be companions and friends.

Throughout my thirty years as an art dealer, people have asked me questions about money. To put it plainly: Is art a good investment? Do auctions provide a good return? How can I sell a work of art I bought many years ago, which I've simply gotten tired of, in the hope that I will at least get what I spent for it?

I'll begin with investment. New collectors are understandably apprehensive when they buy their first works of art, par-

Fernando Botero: *Standing Figure*,
Bronze, 1985, 23 × 9½ × 10"
Courtesy of: James Goodman Gallery, New York

Elizabeth Blackadder: *Longiflorum Lillies*,
Watercolor, 1996, 30 × 20.5"
Courtesy of: Mercury Gallery, London

ticularly if a given piece turns out to be more costly than they anticipated. Of course people do buy art as an investment, but many will deny it, asserting almost defensively that they only bought their works because they loved them. That's the best reason, to be sure, but it's normal to hope that an expensive artwork—a Cubist etching by Braque, for example— will eventually increase in value. When it comes to great works by great masters, there's too much money involved to ignore, even if you are very rich. It's said that the late Nelson Rockefeller, an avid collector, once remarked he would pay up to $10,000 for anything he liked, but beyond that price he wanted to feel sure that he'd get his money back if he sold the piece. Of course Rockefeller made his statement at a time when $10,000 was worth more than it is today.

Well, I'm not in the Rockefeller class, but I still follow my taste and often buy the work of an unknown artist simply because it attracts me. I don't think of such a purchase as an investment, but when I dig deep in my pocket for a piece, you may be certain that I think the piece will be more valuable over time. I wonder why there is a mysterious taboo about mixing esthetics and business. Maybe it has something to do with the notion that religion and commerce can't coexist— yet at a church there is always a collection box and without it a house of worship could not survive. Suffice it to say that in buying art, the finer your feeling for esthetic values grows, the more costly the works you like will turn out to be: as you learn to distinguish between the greater and the inferior work, you'll certainly wind up paying a lot of money for the best. And it is entirely unrealistic to discount the investment.

I'm an art dealer as well as a collector, which means I buy art and try to sell it at a profit. I spend a substantial amount of my money on a given work of art. To justify the expense, I check its provenance, validate its quality, assure myself of its authentication. But the piece is mine until I sell it. It must be something I love, because if it doesn't sell shortly after I buy it, because of a market turn-down, I must be convinced of its quality and happy to live with it. The art market, like the stock market, is subject to mysterious ups and downs just like fashion. As I have said above, the quality of a work of art almost always determines its commercial value—and this whole book is about recognizing quality.

There are people who have to sell when the market dips as it did in the early nineties. The people who have the money buy paintings and sculpture when the market dips and know to buy only the very finest work of the artists they like: a true collector loves art and doesn't just collect signatures. But there are also people who state openly, "I want to invest in art, and I only want big names. I don't know much about art, but I've been told you can quadruple your money with a big-name artist, and I want to be in on the action." To those, my reply is, "It doesn't always work out that way with art, try the stock market instead—that's strictly a matter of investing, and you don't have to look at your mistakes."

People of the latter type are speculators, not at all interested in the art. That's OK, as long as they acknowledge it honestly. The trouble is that in a very short time—usually too short a time—the speculator will want to deal in and out of the art market the way he deals in the stock market, and if he doesn't make his zillion-dollar short-term profit, he is absolutely certain he's been given a bad deal. Speculators—and there were a lot of them in the eighties—are almost always disappointed by the art market. Art, after all, is not soybean futures, pork bellies or junk bonds.

Lester Johnson: *Street Scene*,
Mixed media, 1973, 34½ × 22¾"
Courtesy of: Mr. and Mrs. Charles Kiernan, Connecticut

My next topic involves the so-called lesser known artists. In each century there are only a very limited number of great artists—innovators who see beyond prevailing tastes and techniques, and create radical and permanent changes in the way art is perceived. There were any number of artists who worked at the same time as the French and American Impressionists, the Cubists, the American Hudson River School, the Abstract Impressionist and so on, who were either not as fundamentally original as the famous names or for no apparent reason were just left behind in their own time and only achieved recognition for their work decades after their deaths. These artists worked quietly in relative obscurity. True, many of them had collectors devoted to their work, but often they were not promoted by art galleries. In American painting and sculpture of the thirties and forties, there were many wonderful artists who even today are not yet widely known such as Lester Johnson and Jim Bird. If you like a particular period in American art, look for the best work by the less famous artists who worked then. Prices for lesser known artists are considerably lower, and if you let your sense of quality be your guide you won't make a mistake.

The suggestion goes as well for the artists of our time. The late twentieth century has been a confusing period in the art world. The incredibly original, unique, innovative work executed in the first three-quarters of the century, from Cubism through Constructivism, Abstract Expressionism, Pop, Minimalism and so on, work which changed forever the very definition of fine art, seemed to lose momentum in the eighties. We were witness then to pure hype. Some of those young, ambitious, heavily promoted painters and sculptors will barely be footnotes in art history. Today the work of many of the "stars" of the eighties seldom comes up at auction, because the dealers, sadder but wiser, know it will bomb. And what does a dealer say to a client who bought an astronomically priced piece ten years ago, knowing that the client will never sell it for more than a small fraction of its original price, if he can sell it at all?

168

What with all of the flash artists and dealers who worked in the eighties, there were still many sincere dealers and very talented sculptors, painters and graphic artists who managed to avoid the hype and turn out splendid work. I think we're in a wonderful period for collecting art. The hype and speculation are gone, new artists with genuine vision are emerging, and the work of previously unsung artists is being rediscovered.

Thirty years ago I saw a silverpoint drawing by Manuel Ayaso, a Spanish artist, and fell in love with it. The drawings are small and exquisitely executed, but they aren't easy, happy pictures, and although Ayaso's work has been bought by museums, his audience is not large. No gallery can get rich or manage its overhead on small drawings of living artists. Of course I think Ayaso is a twentieth-century Rembrandt—so you see every good artist eventually finds believers in his or her affirmation of him- or herself.

⁓

If you have started collecting art, you will have to deal with the appraisal of your collection. Appraisal—an expert's estimate of the value of your collection—is important first when you seek to insure the works. And of course if you decide to sell, you'll need an accurate appraisal of a given work's value in today's art market.

If you are selling a work by a contemporary artist, go first to the dealer from whom you bought the piece. He or she should be willing to tell you if the artist's prices have gone up or down at the present time. If the contemporary artist in question is part of the dealer's "stable," the dealer isn't likely to buy it back unless it's an early work: after all, he gets new work directly and exclusively from the artist. In that case you should consult a private dealer who has no direct access to the artist's current work, but is knowledgeable about his earlier pieces and may be the one to sell it for you.

If the piece you want to sell is by a Famous Dead Artist, you have a few useful options. First, look in *Mayer's International Auction Records*, a yearly updated edition of which you can usually find at any large library (and, today, on the Internet). This will give you the last auction price commanded by a work of your artist. If the work is a graphic, consult the yearly updated *Martin Gordon Print Price Annual*. Check whether the work you own by the same artist was done at about the same time as the work listed in *Mayer*, if your piece is about the same size and condition and so on. This research will give you at least a ballpark figure of the current worth of your piece.

If the art you wish to sell is really costly, I suggest you consult a professional appraiser. The appraiser will charge you a fee, but he or she has no personal stake in your work and will give you an honest figure: the fee you pay the appraiser will be more than compensated when you go to sell your art and you have a solid notion of its real worth.

⌒

Armed with your appraisal, you have the option of approaching the auction houses with the work you want to sell, or discussing it with a dealer. Putting a work of art up at auction can be very successful, but you take your chances. You start by putting a reserve on the piece you're selling. The reserve is the amount you will take for the piece, less insurance, the cost of having the auction house reproduce it in its catalogue and the house's own commission (these are hefty figures; be sure to ask the price of the reproduction in the catalogue and the insurance). In the event that the work doesn't sell for the reserve, it is bought in, or bought back, meaning that it's in your hands again. In art jargon, your piece has been burned. The work has been shown in the auction gallery's catalogue, and a great many knowledgeable people, potential buyers, have seen it. They also know the art didn't make its reserve price, and they are going to be suspicious of it after the auction. What was wrong with it? And now if anyone wants it after the auction, they will offer a price way below your reserve and expenses.

If you don't reach the reserve price at auction, the best thing you can do is give the work to a private dealer, who will sell it quietly (for less than the auction price of course), so at least you'll recoup some of your money, or you can hold the piece for a few years in the hope that everyone in the art world will have forgotten it was "burned" at auction.

As I have said before, auction houses can be a trap for the unwary. If you have a well-known, very desirable work of art to sell at auction, advance word of its pending sale will certainly have gotten out throughout the art world, and the auction house will have displayed it before the sale. Deep-pocket collectors and museums will already know about the piece before the auction begins, and with luck, the price of your work may go over the moon.

But auctions are always a gamble, even if you're selling a million-dollar Matisse. The fee charged by the auction house is substantial, but negotiable: for example, if you are selling an entire collection of art, the fee will generally be less than if you are offering only one or two pieces. And in rare cases involving a great work which didn't meet its reserve and was bought in, no fee will be charged: the auction house may pay you the reserve amount which means now they own it, and decide to sit on the artwork until it appreciates in value. But these deals are rare. They happen only when an auction house wants the work badly and is competing with another auction house, or with a powerful dealer, for very expensive works or whole collections.

When it comes to bidding on very rare, expensive artworks at auction, I advise you to retain a dealer or an experienced professional bidder to bid for you. In the auction room you will be up against ferocious competition, people who know the art market inside and out. The auctioner is bidding not only for the owner, but for his company's commission when the hammer comes down. Professional dealers, bidding for you, must charge you a fee for their time, but they can save you from terribly costly mistakes in the auction room. They know the territory.

Above all, don't walk into an art auction, see something you like, and impulsively raise your hand to bid on it because no one else in the room is bidding. Maybe you think you will get a bargain. The piece is presented by the auctioneer below its low estimate in the catalogue, so you assume it's a bargain. *Wrong!* There's a reason the truly knowledgeable aren't bidding it up. Maybe the provenance is questionable, perhaps the piece is not in good condition, or it may be a bad work by a good artist. You must *always* examine works at auction during the days they are displayed before the actual sale, and in the cases of costly oil paintings you should bring in a restorer or conservator to submit the work you like to a thorough examination. If the painting is already valued in the millions by the auction gallery, the gallery's own art experts should not object if you bring in your own. It is certainly not in the auction gallery's interest to sell questionable master-works.

⌒

172

You may well question my lack of enthusiasm for buying or selling at auction. You already know that I am a private dealer, and of course the grand auction galleries compete with me and with art dealers in general. But there are distinct advantages in buying from a dealer. A dealer is a professional who can advise you about a given artwork's quality, condition, provenance and, of course, price—whether the price is too high or too big a "bargain," and whether or not you ought to go for it. Although auction houses began as relatively simple institutions which auctioned off work owned by other people, today they are big corporations with a corporation mentality, often owning the work they sell.

There are periods when a particulary fine artist is in fash-ion and a day comes when without warning he goes out of fashion temporarily. A case in point is Jean Dubuffet, one of the rare artists who comes along from time to time and electrifies the art world. I bought my first Dubuffet drawing in 1971, from a small gallery in Paris. At the time he was executing his "bowery people" and "potato heads." The work I chose was exciting, and I paid very little for it. But then came the eighties, and the Dubuffet market went through the roof. Not only serious collectors, but art spec-ulators as well, were buying all the Dubuffets they could get their hands on, hoping to manipulate the price of his work. Suddenly there were Dubuffets everywhere—and abruptly, his prices plummeted. Whether they had been artifically pushed too high, or whether there was simply too much of his work around and people got tired of it, I don't know.

But when you have the work of an exceptional artist whose name is on everyone's lips and there comes a "hiatus," you can rest easy, his work will be back.

I have a theory about sudden fads in the art world which is directly tied to the economic mood of society. In boom times, when people are optimistic, even overconfident, they are excited by the innovative, the unknown, the *new* in art, and are willing to take risks on untried work. But when the economy takes a downturn, as it did in the early nineties, people feel insecure and prefer art that makes them feel comfortable: the familiar, the recognizable landscape, portrait or vase of flowers, images which make them remember better times. Still, challenging, innovative work eventually reengages the buying public's imagination as society takes another shift into optimism. Indeed, the fading of a fad is ultimately good not only for the collectors of the artist's work, but for the health of the art market in general. The prices of the work of a fine artist will come back, yet the second time around people will pay them not just to get on an overhyped bandwagon, but because they have come to see him or her as an important artist with a solid place in art history.

In other words, don't forego a work of art you love even if you think it may be overpriced by today's market standards. If it's quality work, the market value will eventually catch up. But I don't suggest you buy an expensive work as an investment assuming you'll make money on it. Its price can as easily go down while you are waiting for your killing—and if you didn't love the work for itself when you bought it, you'll be stuck with something you don't want to live with, especially since it will remind you of your mistake.

There are artists whose work is valued more in their own countries than outside them. For example, South Americans and Mexicans love the work of their native artists and pay high prices for it. One can buy a Tamayo more easily, and for less money, in the United States than in Mexico. In Canada, too, the work of the "Group of Seven" is highly esteemed and high priced, though in the States and in Europe few people have heard of them. When it comes to the English artist William Scott, buy his work in America, if you can find it, but sell it in England, where Scott is prized. If a quality work by a foreign artist is offered by your dealer in this country, ask about the prices the artist's work commmands in his or her homeland: this knowledge will prove valuable if you ever want to sell it. Once again, a smattering of knowledge and a touch of economic reality is the best guide.

To sum up: first decide how much money you will honestly feel comfortable spending for a work of art. That assessment will give you a firm idea of what works are available to you. Second, let your own taste be your guide. If a wonderful graphic by a "name artist" is offered for roughly the same price as a mediocre watercolor or oil by the same artist (and remember, even Picaso had off days), go for the best, the wonderful every time—otherwise you are only buying an autograph. And, by all means, take chances on young artists if their work isn't overhyped. The unknown painter whose work you fall in love with when she has her first show in your local gallery just might become world famous—but even if she doesn't, if the work delights you every time you see it on your wall, well, you've given yourself a gift. I would like to mention many wonderful artists but this book has been written to help you discover art wherever you find it, and to provide a little guidance out of my own experience when you begin to buy things you love. None of my opinions are written in stone: I only hope that I have assisted you in developing your own taste and acquiring enough confidence in that taste to proceed happily on a journey in art which will bring you in-finite delight.

175

Selected Bibliography

Ashton, Dore. *The New York School: A Cultural Reckoning.* New York: Penguin Books, 1979.

Casson, Stanley. *XXth Century Sculptors.* Freeport, New York: Books for Libraries Press, 1967.

Coremans, Dr. P.B. *Van Meegeren's Faked Vermeers and De Hooghs:* A Scientific Explanation. Amsterdam: J. M. Meulenhoff, 1949.

Craven, Wayne. *Sculpture in America.* New York: Cornwall Books, 1984.

Diamonstein, Barbralee. *Inside New York's Art World.* New York: Rizzoli, 1979.

Elsen, Albert E. *Origins of Modern Sculpture: Pioneers and Premises.* New York: George Braziller, 1974.

Hamilton, George Heard. *Painting and Sculpture in Europe, 1880-1940.* Baltimore: Penguin Books, 1967.

Hanson, Laurence and Elizabeth Hanson. *Impressionism.* New York: Holt, Rinehart and Winston, 1961.

Hoving, Thomas. *Making the Mummies Dance: Inside the Metropolitan Museum of Art.* New York: Simon and Schuster, 1993.

178 | Irving, Clifford. *Fake: The Story of Elmyr de Hory, the Greatest Art Forger of Our Time.* New York: McGraw-Hill, 1969.

Kingsley, April. *The Turning Point: The Abstract Expressionists and the Transformation of American Art.* New York: Simon and Schuster, 1992.

Lord, James. *Giacometti,* a Biography. New York: Farrar, Straus & Giroux, 1985.

Osborne, Harold, *ed. The Oxford Companion to 20th Century Art.* New York: Oxford University Press, 1981.

Read, Herbert. *The Art of Sculpture.* New York: Princeton University Press, 1956.

Rewald, John. *The History of Impressionism.* 4th ed., rev. New York: Museum of Modern Art, 1973.

———— *Post-Impressionism.* 3rd ed. New York: Museum of Modern Art, 1978.

Rickey, George. *Constructivism – Origins and Evolution.* New York: George Braziller, 1967.

Rose, Barbara. "A.B.C. Art." *Art in America* (October/November 1965).

BIBLIOGRAPHY

Rosenberg, Harold. *Art on the Edge: Creators and Situations.* Chicago: University of Chicago Press, 1975.

Sandler, Irving. *The New York School – Painters & Sculptors of the 50's.* New York: Harper & Row, 1978.